BIG
KNIFE
"Kibugita"

BIG
KNIFE
"Kibugita"

Operating for God in Africa

By Frank Ogden, MD

XULON PRESS

Xulon Press
2301 Lucien Way #415
Maitland, FL 32751
407.339.4217
www.xulonpress.com

Paperback ISBN-13: 978-1-6628-2232-2
Ebook ISBN-13: 978-1-6628-2233-9

DEDICATION

This book is dedicated to my children
Bill, Wes, and Ronda,
who shared many of these experiences
with me in Africa.

CONTENTS

MAP

FOREWORD

"The Kingdom of heaven is like a mustard seed, which a man took and sowed in his field; and this is smaller than all other seeds, but when it is full grown, it is larger than the garden plants and becomes a tree, so that the THE BIRDS OF THE AIR COME and NEST IN ITS BRANCHES."

(Matthew 13:31-32, NASB)

This is the incredible story of the miraculous growth of the Kingdom at Kibuye Hospital in the upcountry of Burundi, Africa, and a faithful servant, Dr. Frank Ogden. If you visited Kibuye Hospital today you would find it buzzing with well-trained doctors and staff. You could tour a thriving medical facility with over 300 beds.

Fifty years ago no one could have imagined this. The surgery center was primitive. The Frank Ogden School of Medicine did not exist. Electricity was not reliable. But the power and presence of the Kingdom was absolutely active – and growing.

The needs of the surrounding population were profound and never ending. Dr. Ogden provided medical care and compassion. To get up at 1:00 a.m. to help someone in crisis was not uncommon. I have heard him say that when a patient came in too late for cure, all he could offer was eternal life with Christ.

The miracle at Kibuye Hospital was sustained by faithful obedience. Dr. Ogden is for us today, a living example of what Eugene Peterson calls "a long obedience in the same direction." This kind of obedience over 43 years and three civil wars comes from a heart of love. We also see in Dr. Ogden, through these pages, evidence of a deep and abiding joy.

I have witnessed that joy many times, watching Dr. Ogden speak about the work with a twinkle in his eye and a smile on his face. It is not an exaggeration to say that he is fueled by the joy of the Holy Spirit of the living God. My wife Shelly and I have had the special privilege of meeting with Frank and Carol for more than ten years, whenever we are both in town. We spend time in conversation, study and prayer. They are models to us. We have been so enriched by their love, support and prayer.

What began 43 years ago as a mustard seed call to obedience and selfless service has helped to grow the work at what is now Kibuye Hope Hospital, a major medical service and training center. Hundreds of lives have been changed. Thousands have found healing, both physically and spiritually. Many are in heaven today as a result of this obedient servant and this wonderful work.

Dr. and Mrs. Ogden not only served the medical and spiritual needs of Burundian people, they drew many others into the work. In this wonderful way, he was sowing the seeds of the Kingdom in our lives.

May the Lord inspire you as you read these pages, and may we too live lives of faithful obedience, love and service.

David Goodnight, J.D., LL.M.

PREFACE

This story of my life, spanning eight and half decades, shows many opportunities for service as well as travel around the world; but I want it to emphasize how God has blessed me (with wife Maxine and then Carol) because of our commitment to Him. When I was unable to take the exam to be board certified in General Surgery, God provided another avenue to complete my residency at a different hospital. That's where I received even better surgical training that particularly helped me as a surgeon heading for developing countries. Being awarded the Humanitarian of the Year in 2011 by my alma mater, the University Of Washington School Of Medicine, made up for the lack of the other certification.

This is the account of my preparation for missionary service and the medical adventures I had in the development of rural hospitals in three Central African countries.* But more than that, it is the story of how God advances His cause through committed servants of Christ, using medicine to relieve physical suffering and pointing people to Christ.

I am grateful for all the time and effort given by my wife, Carol, who has helped me in the writing and editing of this book.

*Since the map shows the three hospitals I refer to throughout the book, I have usually left off the country name in the text. They are:

- Kibuye Hospital, Burundi (which later became Kibuye Hope Hospital (KHH)
- Kibogora Hospital, Rwanda
- Nundu Deaconess Hospital, Democratic Republic of Congo (DRC), which I sometimes refer to by its earlier name of Zaire.

INTRODUCTION

In 1970 I first arrived in Burundi to serve at Kibuye Hospital with my wife Maxine and three children. I was following several doctors who had served before me since 1946 when the hospital first opened, chiefly, Dr. Esther Kuhn, the founder, and later Dr. Len Ensign. Others came for short or long periods—builders, evangelists, educators, medical personnel. I am grateful for the service of these men and women who paved the way for me starting way back in 1935 when Rev. J.W. Haley, the first Free Methodist missionary arrived in Central Africa. He drove all the way from South Africa which was not an easy feat in those days. He was joined by Paul and Estelle Orcutt who started the Kibuye mission station. They were pioneers in every sense of the word.

What we found on arrival at Kibuye was a 42-bed hospital with a small but dedicated staff. The nurses who worked closely with me were Doris Moore (Meredith), RN from Canada, Lydia Bimenyimana, nurse; Sophonie Batwenga, nurse anesthetist, and Andre Minani, Operating Room (OR) assistant. We had basic equipment with which to do medicine and surgery—a portable x-ray machine and a generator to power electric lights in the operating room. Kerosene lanterns were important for night duty in the wards. The water supply was usually good, though sometimes lacking. The pharmacy had basic medicines most of the time. We didn't have fancy facilities and medicines; but God was with us, helping us meet the challenges.

I plugged right in to building up services for the years ahead, while doing my best to serve a population of 250,000. Later my African staff nicknamed me *Kibugita,* meaning Big Knife in both Kinyarwanda and Kirundi, the languages of Rwanda and Burundi. The reason for this name is explained in chapter seven.

Since the road was only paved part way from the capital city of Bujumbura, our 100 mile journey to Kibuye was an all-day event, especially in rainy season. Nowadays it takes two and a quarter hours.

In the early days there was no blood available, so I had to devise a way to take it from a patient and store it until his operation two weeks later, in order to give it back to him. Being the only surgeon I was quite busy caring for every kind of illness. Often people came from a far distance, even adjacent countries such as Tanzania and Congo. Epidemic typhus was a devastating epidemic. We had nearly one hundred percent fatality rate until I learned that one 100 mg tablet of doxycycline would cure it.

Though I was absent for some years Dr. Dave Crandall, a general surgeon, began building the new hospital at Kibuye in 1973. When I returned three years later, I completed the construction and appreciated working in this much larger facility with two operating rooms, maternity, wards, lab and pharmacy. In 1990 I started the feeding program called Busoma (see chapter 7) to prevent the malnutrition of children. This has since grown into a major nutrition program, with the help of Free Methodist International Childcare Ministry (ICCM) and other donors.

There were some setbacks along the way. Two civil wars in Burundi (1972 & 1993) took the lives of many hospital staff, and caused others to flee. Along with the terrible loss of medical personnel, hospital buildings and supplies were devastated. However, God continued to bless Kibuye through the troubled times, enabling faithful staff to offer healthcare and hope to thousands of people.

Another devastating blow was losing my wife of 39 years after battling colon cancer for three years. I wondered how I could continue to work at Kibuye without her. Then in June 1997 the Lord gave me a new helpmate. Carol Watson had been an evangelistic missionary for ten years in Rwanda prior to the genocide of that country. We were already somewhat acquainted, both serving with Free Methodist World Missions. Together we continued to serve the hospital and the church full time until 2005, when I retired just short of age seventy.

Returning to Kibuye on a short-term volunteer basis, I was able to help train the first class of medical students who came through the program named after me. It was thrilling to attend their graduation in December 2012.

When I finally hung up my scalpel in early 2013, we left a one hundred thirty bed hospital as a referral center for ten health centers. A team of young doctors was coming later that year to continue the work in the highlands of central Burundi. God gave me a glimpse of the bright future this team would bring to the hospital where I had worked for over a period of five decades.

Chapter 1

EARLY YEARS

"Now boys, don't you go playing near that cistern," Mama reminded us. I was five years old, living in a parsonage in Cloverland, Washington. Just outside the back porch we had a cistern—a tank in the ground—filled with water which was trucked over by a neighbor. Philip, who was only about three at the time, couldn't resist. He got up on the lid, which was not tightly closed; it dumped him right into that cistern. My youngest brother nearly drowned, and I was watching from a tree across the yard. Our other brother Milton was near the cistern. It was he who raised the alarm.

"Philip's in the cistern!" he shouted, running into the house. Good thing Mama was resourceful, even under stress. She took a garden rake and fished out her little boy by hooking his clothing. After he was safely in the house, swaddled in a towel, I finally got to the kitchen door.

"I —was—comin'–to—tell you—Mama." After all, it takes time to get down from a thorny locust tree! Apparently, I was slow enough at certain things that for a while my folks thought I was not very bright. Fortunately, all four of us turned out just fine; and we always said Phil, the one who nearly drowned, was the smartest. (He got his PhD in Nuclear Physics and had a forty-year career as a professor at Roberts Wesleyan

College in Rochester, New York.) We have all thanked God for preserving his life that day.

I was born September 28, 1935 in Caldwell, Idaho, the second child and eldest son of Rev. Horatio W. and Wilma E. Ogden. My siblings are:

- Myrtle, born 5/25/1933 (married Don Moller). She died of cancer on 11/11/2009
- Milton, born 11/05/1936 (married Karolyn Schneider)
- Philip, born 02/03/1938 (married Edna Mudge and after her death, Judy Brandenburg)

At two weeks of age I was taken to worship in the Free Methodist Church (FMC) of Deer Flat, Idaho where my father was the pastor. My parents were Godly examples to me, leading us in family prayer and Bible reading, so I came to know the way of Christ early in life.

At age six at a meeting at an FM church in Spokane I knelt at the altar to ask Jesus into my heart. As I grew older my faith increased. I clearly remember my mother reading to us four children about missionaries of the past. I especially liked the stories of pioneer missionaries to Africa, such as Dr. David Livingstone and his father-in-law, Robert Moffatt. Little did I know that God was working in my heart through these stories, so that I would later hear His call to serve as a missionary doctor to Africa.

My Swedish Grandfather

Franz Gustav Carlson boarded a ship in his native Sweden in 1891 and came to New York. He was fifteen years old and accompanied by his sister, age twenty-five. They had no knowledge of English, but Frank (as he was known in his new country) was very industrious in learning the new language and culture. One of his jobs was selling door to door for the Fuller Brush Co. An interesting thing happened after the door was opened at one home.

"This fellow would be a good catch," Frank heard the lady of the house tell her daughter in Swedish. He gave his usual sales pitch (in English) and when it came time to leave he said goodbye in Swedish, much to the lady's surprise (and embarrassment!)

In 1900 Frank married Affa Root and together they reared eleven children - six daughters and five sons. Wilma was the third child and married my father in 1931, after teaching grade school for two years in Idaho. She had met Horatio at Seattle Pacific College (SPC). Dad financed his way in college by delivering telegrams for Western Union on his Indian motorcycle.

How my family became Christians

My father, Horatio Wilbur Ogden (who later went by H.W.), was the firstborn of Will and Cora Ogden in Portland, Oregon September 23, 1907. How his family became Christians and joined the Free Methodist denomination is interesting. In the winter of 1913, when he was only six years old the family made a big move east—seven miles from Portland to Gresham. And it was a big move in those days. They had to hire a wagon pulled by a team of horses.

By the time the teamster arrived and all of their household belongings were loaded on the wagon the day was half spent. As it was winter, with snow on the ground and daylight hours limited, it was no surprise that darkness overtook the family by the time they got to the area of their new home.

"I wonder if we're on the right road," Will said to his wife. They were looking for the house outside the town of Gresham, but rural roads had no street lights and they were beginning to wonder if they had missed a turn somewhere. Just then Horatio's parents saw a home with a lighted window—no doubt a kerosene lamp. They stopped at this home to inquire about their destination.

"Yes, you're on the right road," said Mr. Cathey, "but no one is living at that house."

"Yes, I know that," replied Grandpa Will. "You see, we are the new occupants coming to live there."

"It's cold," said Mr. Cathey. "The stovepipe has not been cut. And how will you get your bed assembled in the dark? You must stay the night here with us." So they agreed. The Cathey family fed them, cared for the horses and driver, and found sleeping accommodations for everyone.

The next day they led my grandparents to the house and helped them move in— cutting the stovepipe, putting the bed together, and generally getting settled. That was Saturday and the Catheys invited the Ogdens to church the next day.

Although they were not church goers Will & Cora felt they could not refuse the invitation after all the wonderful help they'd been given. So they went with the

Catheys to the Gresham Free Methodist Church. They were both converted and became members. Grandma went to the altar that very first Sunday.

"Had you ever heard about this Gospel message of Christ?" she asked her husband on the way home. He said he had heard about it but had paid no attention. Grandpa soon followed Grandma in repentance, and so did their little son Horatio (my father). All because of a light in the window on a dark, snowy night!

Later Grandpa and Grandma moved to Avon, Washington (near Mount Vernon) where they ran a dairy farm. Grandpa, with sons Horatio, Don, Ray and Dan, delivered milk in the area. By the time I came along in the family the retail milk delivery was finished and all four sons had left for other employment and rearing of families. The dairy continued. A big truck came and picked up the milk each day. Will and Cora were active in the Free Methodist Church of Mount Vernon which later figures in my story.

Dad becomes a Free Methodist Pastor

After my father graduated from Seattle Pacific College (now University), he was ordained in the Free Methodist Denomination. He pastored two churches before I was born—Daisy and Chewelah, both in eastern Washington. If you've never heard of Daisy it may be because it is now under water due to the construction of Coulee Dam.

Then we went to Deer Flat, Idaho from 1934-38. I was too young to remember the three years I lived in the parsonage there, but I do remember later visits to

Grandpa Carlson's farm. From Deer Flat we moved to the small FMC at Cloverland, Washington. I remember our old '29 Chrysler, brush painted dark red. This is where the cistern incident (at the opening of this chapter) took place.

We had a cow, some chickens and a garden. My sister, Myrtle, three years older than I, started to school just across the road from our little house. She was also a curious child and while still a baby, so we're told, she crawled across the gaveled road to see what those school children were all about. Myrtle is also known to have picked up eggs from the neighbors' porch when they were away, breaking them to see what was inside.

The day we drank beer

Our family's next place of service was Walla Walla, also in eastern Washington. This is where I started first grade, after taking a test because my sixth birthday was late in September. I can well remember what happened one Sunday morning when Dad found some bottles of beer in the front yard of the parsonage. This wasn't surprising since the church was right down town. He decided to give each of us children a taste of beer to show us how terrible it was. Handing us each a spoon, Dad poured some beer into them for us to taste. We spitted it out in disgust, and the lesson worked—I've never touched a drop of liquor since!

Wouldn't you know, that morning we had a temperance lesson in Sunday School and thoroughly embarrassed our parents, not meaning to of course. Just when the teacher finished telling all about the evils of alcohol my brother Phil piped up, "We had beer at our house this morning and Daddy drank some too." That brought down the house, and Mom wanted to crawl under the pew while Dad tried to explain things.

Advantages of being a Pastor's Kid

In those years our denomination moved pastors every three years. That's how I ended up going to eight schools before college. In each new place, it seemed that our parsonage home needed repairs or remodeling. I learned which end of the hammer to use and many other skills helping Dad fix up our houses. When we moved to Plummer, Idaho, Dad taught science in the local high school as well as pastoring.

In his "spare" time he and a parishioner felled trees, pulled them out of the woods with a horse, and loaded them on his truck, to provide us with wood for the cold winters in Northern Idaho. This is when I learned to use a crosscut or buck saw, as my brothers and I spent many hours cutting up the logs. We then split them with a maul and axe. A chainsaw would have helped a lot, but wasn't available then.

The parsonage was attached to the church, so it was easy to have a family hymn sing by going next door. Mother played on the pump organ, and we learned many hymns and gospel songs in that little church. This encouraged all four of us children in our faith. Another bonus was getting a dog, and it happened in an interesting way. One day this red Irish setter came to our front porch and simply adopted us. He would habitually sleep there with our cat sleeping on his back. We named him Chess.

Tragedy on Grandpa's Farm

Several summers two or three of us boys spent time at Grandpa Ogden's dairy farm near Mount Vernon, Washington. I learned to drive his truck while he pitched the loose hay on it. We enjoyed being with Grandpa and felt useful helping on the farm. One day Milt and I were riding on the back of the tractor with Grandpa cutting thistles and other weeds in the pasture. Suddenly the left wheels got too close to the slope going down to the drainage ditch. He shouted *"Jump off!'* and we did. Those are the last words we heard from our Grandpa.

The tractor rolled over, pinning him under water in the drainage ditch. We were appalled. Of course, we ran for help, but it was more than an hour before a wrecker could remove the tractor. Grandpa had no chance of survival. He was only in his sixties. Grandma continued to run the dairy, and we helped her in many ways when we could. For some reason Milt became her favorite, maybe because he was much better at milking than I.

How the war changed our life

In 1945 Dad joined the US Army as a chaplain and was sent to Fort Oglethorpe, Georgia for training. The rest of us moved to Mount Vernon, so we could be near Dad's mother (still running the dairy farm) while he was away. One day we were returning home from a visit to my Carlson grandparents in Idaho. As we drove through Yakima, we noticed cars honking, dragging tin cans, and making a huge racket. "*What's going on Mother*?" It was August of 1945, and she told us the war was over. Our first thought was of Dad, wondering when he would come home. As it turned out he had just finished his training and was assigned transport duty on ships bringing soldiers home, first from Europe, and then from the Pacific. This caused him to be gone for months at a time.

After living in town for a year, with Dad's con-currence, Mom bought an eight-acre place near Little Mountain outside Mount Vernon. Most of it was forest, but it had a three-bedroom house and some cleared area. The Little Mountain Road that ran in front of our house was not yet paved, nor did we have electricity for over a year. A man came and dug a well by hand, then installed a hand pump in the kitchen. We had been used to turning on a faucet, at least in the kitchen. I guess Mom wanted us to learn more life skills that come with living off the land. Little did I know that God was using these new challenges in everyday life to prepare me for later missionary life in Central Africa.

Besides having to light kerosene lamps and pump water we did all our heating and cooking with wood. It's a good thing my brothers and I had learned how to cut wood when living in Plummer. Now I was 11, Milt 10 and Phil 9. Before Grandpa died he had transitioned to a Ford tractor on the farm and we were given his Percheron work horse, Old Babe, who was 20 years old. We three boys felled the trees, and Old Babe dragged them out of the woods. Then, just as we had done in Plummer, we used the crosscut saw to cut them into useable lengths, chop them with the maul & wedges, and stack them for winter in the shed. I made countless trips carrying wood to the kitchen stove or living room fireplace. I found out it takes a lot of wood to heat with an ordinary fireplace and a kitchen stove.

This home in the country also gave us the space to have a cow and chickens, and even goats later on. Myrtle, now old enough to appreciate what was inside eggs, tended to the chickens. We built a special platform for milking the goats. I enjoyed these years. In the summers we rode our bicycles to Skagit flats, some six miles away, to pick strawberries for some cash. Then we'd have to ride back, a lot of it uphill, after picking all day in sun or rain. I attended the fifth, sixth, and seventh grades at Lincoln School in Mount Vernon.

While Dad was away on active duty he wrote us letters regularly, giving all the news of his life aboard ship. Maybe that's how I acquired the habit of writing to family back home once I was in Africa for months and years at a time.

One time during a storm in the Pacific Dad's troop ship lurched just as he was carrying a typewriter up a ladder. He grabbed the typewriter to keep it from falling and injured his back. This resulted in his stay at Letterman Army Hospital in San Francisco for a number of months. Now his communication included phone calls, and then we got to see him when he came home once during his convalescence.

Chapter 2

SCHOOL DAYS

Dad got out of the Army and returned home in 1948. The Free Methodist Conference asked him to move to Tacoma, Washington to pastor the McKinley Park Church. I attended Gault Junior High for Grades eight and nine and then went on to Lincoln High School for tenth grade. I took Latin that year, which helped me with both English grammar and in learning French which I began the following year.

Dad's next assignment was Buckley FMC & I attended White River High School for my junior year. Latin was not offered here so I switched to French (which later helped me as a missionary in French-speaking Africa). However, my teacher, just out of college, did not press us very hard, so I didn't feel that I made much progress.

My third high school was in Richland, Washington since Dad reenlisted in the Army in 1952 and was stationed at Camp Hanford. We moved into a house in nearby Kennewick, but since we three boys had friends in Richland (just across the Yakima River) we were allowed to drive ourselves to Columbia High School in Richland. We attended the Free Methodist Church in Richland and I enjoyed working alongside the men as we helped finish the church building. My brothers and I learned a lot about construction that year, another way the Lord was preparing me for missionary service in rural Africa. Little did I imagine how much I would put these skills to work in future years.

This school had a very good French teacher, so the second-year class was far above my level coming from Buckley. I had to really scratch to catch up, and I learned a lot of French which became important later as I needed it in Africa. In winter we drove many times in our '41 Plymouth on frosty roads with either Milt or me having our head out the window watching the fog line, because the heater was not able to clear the windshield.

More than Academics

Besides construction skills and French language acquisition, I also had my first opportunity to fly in a small plane during my senior year. It was with my mother's cousin, Merle Root, who lived in Prosser at the time—a town about 20 miles away. It was exciting coming in right over the trees to the small airfield at Prosser. Later I got my own pilot's license and became a flight surgeon in the Army. (see Appendix 3.) Cousin Merle & his wife Beulah also livened up some Friday nights by inviting the church young people to their place for movies—16mm films checked out from the library.

Another interesting happening during my senior year was that I learned to use a 22-gauge rifle. Our favorite sport at this time was shooting rabbits and I have to say they are very hard to hit with a 22! One rabbit hunting expedition stands out in my mind.

We three boys left the house at 5AM in order to reach the Horse Heaven Hills near Kennewick at sunrise. However, a large rabbit ran across the road one block from home, so we loaded our rifle to go after it. Before we opened the door a car came out of the darkness and stopped alongside. It was a deputy sheriff. *Oh no!* We knew it was not legal to have our gun loaded in the car or to hunt at night. *Wow! Are we in trouble?* We quickly explained that we were going rabbit hunting in the hills.

"How would you like to go with me to the dump and shoot rats instead?" asked the officer. We were so relieved at his response. He never mentioned the state of our weapons. (The rabbit was long gone by this time.) *Wow!* That sounded a lot better than being hauled to the police station. *OK!* All three of us agreed. The dump was just a few blocks away, so we followed him there.

Using the bright spotlight of the patrol car to illuminate our surroundings he showed us some pretty good marksmanship with his 38 revolver. I am not sure how many rats were hit, as they soon disappeared after the first shots were fired, but our new "friend" was quite good at hitting pop cans at 20 to 30 yards. I don't remember if the rest of us fired any bullets or not, but we were surely amazed at this officer's ability.

Impressing Girls

My brother Milt and I bought our first car, a '36 Chev 2-door sedan. It had some trouble, including the universal joint which caught on fire once. We threw dirt on the U-joint to put out the fire. This happened when we were in Burlington, and we somehow lubricated it enough to drive back to Kennewick and replace the U-joint there. Because of these problems with the

Chev we bought a '41 Plymouth. That old Plymouth was interesting also. The accelerator had the habit of sticking on the floorboard; thus, in order to stop the engine roaring we had to turn off the ignition before releasing the clutch and reach down to pull the accelerator pedal back up.

This caused backfiring for several seconds and blew the side out of the muffler. It then sounded like a truck, but that didn't bother us. One day at Burlington Camp the youth were playing volley ball, so Milt and I drove up close to where they were playing and intentionally caused this backfiring. This was for the benefit of our friends, especially to impress the girls. To our surprise this caused the dry grass underneath the car to ignite, so Milt quickly restarted the engine; and before it revved too much moved the car away from the fire. We later fixed the spring on the accelerator and installed a new muffler. That car travelled many miles for us.

On to College

It sounds like I only had extra-curricular activities during my senior year, but actually, my studies went very well and I graduated in 1953 from high school with honors. After that I went to Mount Vernon to work on my grandmother's farm for the summer. Milt was with me. We harvested hay and took care of the cows. We worked nights at the frozen food plant in nearby Avon packing strawberries or blackberries. That September I enrolled in SPC, my parents' alma mater. At the same time the Army sent Dad to Korea as the Korean War was coming to an end. He was there when prisoners were being exchanged. The family moved back to the house on Little Mountain outside Mount Vernon, but I started at Seattle Pacific College. I lived in Alexander Hall with Ron Ensign, my friend from Richland, as roommate.

Besides working hard to graduate with honors to be accepted into medical school and working part-time in the evenings, I also made time to have some fun. During my senior year at Seattle Pacific I was the head of the campus blood drive. To advertise the upcoming event we had a few moments to present during morning chapel in McKinley Auditorium. While I was speaking about donating blood a friend staggered down the aisle and collapsed just below the platform. My helpers rushed down with a stretcher and brought him up on the platform and onto a table.

We wheeled in a blood donor on a gurney, who had hidden under his shirt a hot water bottle filled with raspberry Kool-Aid. The victim had a hot water bottle under his shirt, too. By attaching plastic tubing between the two we were able to put pressure on the donor's chest and the 'blood' flowed from him to the victim. The victim promptly got up and smiled, thanking us and walked off the stage. However, several in the audience had trouble with their stomachs, but I don't think anyone fainted. The whole thing was a great success, and we got plenty of blood donors.

God's Call to Missionary Service

Anatomy and Physiology proved to be a pivotal class in my freshman year. I liked it; did well in it; and felt in a special way that I could serve God in missions as a doctor and surgeon. When I had felt God calling me to missions in high school, I had told Him, "*I can't do that. I'm not good at public speaking.*" I could not see myself in pastoral/evangelistic ministry. But now I could see how I might fulfill this calling, so that became my goal through college, medical school and training in surgery.

Though I was in a general surgery program, I was able to also get training in gynecology, urology, ortho-pedics, maxillo-facial, and plastic surgery. These were all very useful things, as much of the time in Africa I had no other specialists with me. Prior to going to Burundi in 1970 I studied Tropical Medicine at Tulane University in New Orleans, Louisiana,

Missionary service was not a new thought to me. I come from a missionary-minded family. My parents applied to our denomination's mission board soon after they married; but they were told that there was no money, as it was the middle of the Depression. Later they reapplied and were told, "You have too many children."(four). Instead, they served the Lord through pastoral and chaplaincy ministry, and later, by supporting me in my missionary career.

Chapter 3
MARRIAGE, MEDICAL SCHOOL & UNCLE SAM

Early in my senior year at SPC I noticed a pretty young lady walking across the campus the same hour each day, so I fell in step with her and began a conversation. She was Maxine Harer, the daughter of our FM pastor in Bremerton. After taking classes for one year, she was now working full time in the Education Department as the secretary for Vivian Larsen. Maxine lodged in the home of Dr .and Mrs. Harold Wiebe who lived at the edge of campus. As I walked her home that day I asked her for a date.

Maxine had grown up as a PK (Preacher's Kid) like me, so we had a similar background–hard work, moving a lot and living in parsonages that often needed remodeling. We both understood the little poem "Make it do; Wear it out; Use it up; Do without." These values were an asset to us in later years as we set up house together in rural Africa. Also, being in the same denomination, we shared experiences related to District Meeting, Annual Conference and Camp Meeting.

That first date developed into a courtship throughout my senior year. Our relationship developed quickly. It was winter. While playing in the snow, I asked Maxine,

"Could you see yourself as a missionary?"

I was very happy when she answered, "Yes!" The next evening I borrowed Vince Spencer's '53 Pontiac (much nicer than my '49 Plymouth with rusted floor boards) and drove my sweetheart to Golden Gardens Park in the suburbs of Seattle. By now the snow had melted, so we took a path up into the woods. It was totally dark, and I asked Maxine to be my wife. Of course, she agreed, and we started making wedding plans for June.

Ogden brothers Phil, Frank & Milt, 1954

Frank's parents, HW & Wilma Ogden with Maxine & FO, 1957

Maxine & FO with first child, Billy, 1960

Frank & Maxine Ogden with children from left to right:
Billy, Ronda & Wesley, 1969

On the morning of June 10, 1957, I graduated with
honors with a BS in Zoology, and that same evening
I took Maxine to be my wife. We were married in the
Bremerton FMC with both our fathers performing the
ceremony. The wedding itself went off without a hitch,
but we had a related incident concerning my new brother-in-law, Gerald Harer. He nearly spent the night in jail
for driving around the block without his car lights on,
getting ready for the wedding chase. Fortunately, Dr.
Fred Drew was able to talk the cops out of arresting
him. You might wonder why we would plan our wedding on the same day as graduation. For one thing, the
bride herself was not graduating and secondly, it was

expedient for our family members to be on hand for both ceremonies on the same day.

Starting our Honeymoon with Mom and Dad

Maxine and I had a very unusual honeymoon following our first night in a Federal Way motel. Since my father was needing to return to his Army assignment at Fort Shafter, Hawaii, it was decided that Maxine and I would drive Mom, Dad & Phil to San Francisco to catch a military plane to Honolulu. Maybe this seems like a strange start to a marriage, but in those days it made sense to help the family in this way. We used my brother Milt's Mercury sedan and dropped them off at Uncle Wilbur's place in Redwood City. Here they awaited their flight from Travis Air Force Base.

Family helped each other in those days and we didn't think anything about it. Having done our part, Maxine and I headed back to Seattle, stopping for the night in Williams, California. But, wouldn't you know, the horse show in town had taken all the good motel rooms. All we could find was a tiny room in a "flea-bag" motel, a far cry from a bridal suite. But it only cost $4 and we survived.

Medical School Memories

Before graduating I had applied to four medical schools: St. Louis University, Creighton University (Omaha), Stanford University, and University of Washington (UW in Seattle). I had an interview at the UW but received no answer from them. I then received acceptance at Stanford School of Medicine, which is highly regarded in the field. I didn't have to travel to California for the interview, because a professor at the UW was a representative for the Stanford School of Medicine. I told the UW about this acceptance, and therefore I needed their answer within two weeks. This prompted a second interview with the UW, and this time I was accepted. I can't help but wonder if it was my stated goal to be a missionary that had hindered my acceptance earlier. I declined Stanford, choosing to stay at home and attend the University of Washington.

That summer between college and medical school I worked for Seattle's Department of Engineering. I didn't do any engineering, however; my job was parking cars at the city dump! As I conversed with people who brought their loads to the dump it often came up that I was a medical student. Some didn't believe me. Being very enterprising I found a number of things being thrown away that I took home and used to furnish our apartment. I once listed all the items I had "reclaimed" from the dump in a letter to the folks. It included such diverse items as a mailbox, tool box and 8-foot step ladder. I'm sure Maxine was happy to get a free bedroom rug, kitchen chair and ironing board, just to name a few.

This first home of ours was a "free-rent" upstairs apartment of my parents' house at 303 West Dravus, across the street from SPC. As the folks were away in Hawaii, they had rented out the downstairs to Vern & Jeannie Matthews. It was fun to have another young married couple nearby for games and fellowship.

When fall came I began medical school at the UW, a short drive away. I enjoyed the studies and was soon in the upper third of my class. However, my downfall was psychiatry, and I had to repeat it in the summer while working for Seattle City Light. My assignment was in the underground division in which we transferred the power lines underground in downtown Seattle in preparation for the 1962 World's Fair. I really got a tan that summer! The third summer was my favorite—working for the Parks Department. It was much better to set sprinklers, rake leaves and sweep walks than to dig trenches in the hot sun.

Meanwhile, Maxine had found work as a secretary at Boeing which boosted our income. She did this for two years and then started her new job as a *mother*. Our son, William Frank, was born February 1, 1960 at Swedish Hospital in Seattle in the middle of my third year of medical school. He was Billy until he wanted to be called Bill.

In my final year of medical school, I was in a group of five as we rotated through the various services. While on the surgical rotation we operated on dogs. At the time of our last operation we asked the professor if we could do an aortic graft on our dog. He agreed, so we did that rather specialized procedure. Years later, I was able to do this procedure on human patients. I felt I had very good training at the University of Washington.

All five of our group went on to train in surgical specialties—two in orthopedics, one in gynecology, one in plastic surgery, and I in general surgery. It was interesting at our 50 year reunion to reminisce of how we had worked together in our last year of med school.

We're in the Army Now

My Dad found out that senior medical students could join the Army and receive pay as a second lieutenant, so I took his advice and joined up. I didn't have to attend basic training, go to any drills or even wear a uniform until after graduation. With the officer's pay I was able to graduate from medical school with no debts. This was a huge blessing to us as newlyweds, bound for medical missionary service.

Our second son, Wesley Paul, was born June 3, 1961 at Fort Lawton Hospital, Washington since I was in the Army now. One week later Maxine was able to attend my graduation from medical school on June tenth, our fourth wedding anniversary. I was selected by the Army for a rotating internship at Brooke Army Medical Center in San Antonio, Texas. The Army moved our belongings for us, so we only had to pack what we needed for our journey to Texas in our 1960 Vauxhall sedan.

Before leaving on this long journey we visited my parents for a day or two, now pastoring the FMC in Burlington, Washington. As we began loading the car for our big move, going back and forth from the house to the car, Billy, age one and one half, would not stop crying no matter how we tried to console him. Finally we figured out the problem—he was afraid he would be left behind. So we set him in the car and he was fine.

In those days we didn't have car seats for children or seatbelts for anyone, so we were able to pack things on the floor in the back seat, making it level with the bench seat. This gave Billy a flat play area. Wesley, age four weeks, lay content in a cardboard box on the seat beside Billy. There was no air-conditioning in our car, but we made it to San Antonio fine. I was promoted to first lieutenant, and I learned a lot that year as I got to apply what I had learned in medical school while caring for patients on my own.

We bought a 2-bedroom house. Hurricane Carla came near to San Antonio one night and shredded our banana tree. Maxine got up in the night and found Billy looking out the screen door at the devastation in our back yard, but fortunately she grabbed him before he had ideas of going out into the gale. He wasn't even two yet, but he had opened the door himself. No wonder he became an engineer.

At the end of the one year internship we left San Antonio at 8PM on a July evening with 105 degrees. We were heading for Escondido, California for my brother Phil's wedding. We were now driving a '62 Plymouth Variant with no air conditioning. (My first *new* car). We stopped at Lordsburg, New Mexico to sleep for some hours during the day, then drove on during the night when it cooled down a bit, finally reaching our destination the next day. The little boys in the backseat did fine.

I still had three more years to serve in Uncle Sam's Army, so I had applied for training as a flight surgeon (one who looks after the health & safety of pilots). At that time the Army did not have their own flight surgeon school, so I went to the Navy school in Pensacola, Florida for six months. I had a pilot's license before joining the Army, and part of the curriculum at Pensacola was to fly solo in the T-34. I found this very enjoyable. With instructors we were also able to do some aerobatics in the T-28.

During Christmas vacation I was able to fly with a jet instructor pilot, and that was really fun, as they were doing gunnery practice with a tow plane pulling the banner/target. We made repeated runs on the banner pulling as much as five g's. One day as I reported to get my plane, my old friend from grade school days in Idaho spoke to me from behind the counter, *"Frank Ogden!"* It was Dan Corn that I had not seen in almost twenty years. I knew he had gone into the Navy, but I had no idea that he was serving at Pensacola. We renewed our friendship with him and Linda, and they later went to Africa to help us for one year.

My next assignment was the US Army Board for Aviation Accident Research at Fort Rucker, Alabama. The Army, by now, had started their own flight surgeon school, so I taught part time in that school while my main job was studying accidents and development of safety equipment for pilots. Fort Rucker is a training base for helicopter pilots for the Army. Some of my new friends were instructors; and they let me fly the helicopters, though not as solo.

Part of my work was research on accidents due to disorientation in helicopter flying. Tactical flying into sand or snow can be very difficult for pilots, causing them to lose their spatial orientation. I presented my work at the Aerospace Medicine meeting in Miami Beach, Florida and it was published in Aerospace Medicine Magazine.

A memorable experience was flying with Major Carpenter in the Mohawk reconnaissance twin-turbo-prop plane. Probably the most fun was with Captain Cliff Carlberg in the Beavers and L-19s. My instructor was comfortable flying in the right seat, so I learned a lot from him by flying in the pilot's seat on the left. Much of it was instrument instruction, so I would put on the hood just after takeoff and not see anything but the instrument panel until ready to land again. Many times we practiced VOR (Visual Omni Range) instrument approaches to locate the runway.

One time as we were returning to Fort Rucker fog was settling in, obscuring the field, so we called for a GCA (ground-controlled approach). The controller told us exactly when to turn to certain compass headings and descend toward the runway.

"If you do not have visual contact at this time, execute a 'missed approach,'" he said. Disappointed, we knew that meant we'd have to fly to a distant field without fog. However, at that very moment, we descended through the fog and located the runway straight ahead of us and made a good landing. That makes me think about trusting God to bring us through a situation, when we can't see our way. He is the controller of our life, just as the GCA controller led us through the fog that day. (See more airplane stories in Appendix 3.)

Chapter 4
AFRICA, HERE WE COME

Surgical Residency

My colleagues wanted me to stay in the Army, but I knew it was time to move on to surgery training in order to prepare for missionary service. I received a position in general surgery residency at Virginia Mason Hospital (VMH) in Seattle. So our family of four packed up and moved back to Seattle. That was a special year for a number of reasons.

Our daughter, Ronda Kay, was born April 14, 1966 at VMH. Bill entered kindergarten. We bought a house on Queen Anne Hill, and I joined the Evergreen Flying Club. We flew our four-passenger Maule to California to check out a better position in surgery, as I didn't feel I had enough opportunities in surgery at VMH.

I got a position at San Joaquin General Hospital in Stockton for my second year of residency so our family of five moved once again in July 1966. We bought a two acre place in the country and had Shetland ponies.

My third year in California I worked at the affiliated hospital in Modesto named Scenic General. I really got a lot of good experience there–not only in general surgery but also in gynecology, urology, orthopedics and plastic surgery. All this prepared me for future years in Africa.

Doctor at Yosemite

At the conclusion of my training in Modesto I took a summer job at Yosemite National Park treating mostly minor illnesses and injuries. However, one day a lady from a serious auto accident was brought in. We operated and repaired multiple injuries to the small intestine. We later transferred her to a hospital in Merced. Living in the park that summer was interesting for the children because deer and raccoons came often in our yard. Mother raccoon brought her little ones to eat watermelon rinds at our door.

On my days off we went hiking in the high country. Hikes were difficult for little Ronda, age three. We encouraged her with Life Savers as "pep pills". Often Billy or I would carry her, when she was too weary to walk further. We tent camped at night & ran our provisions up a tree to keep them away from bears. In October, as I was finishing my time in Yosemite, my parents drove down from Washington, and we camped together at Tuolumne Meadows at an elevation over 8,000 feet. As you can imagine, the nights were quite chilly.

Mom & Dad were sleeping in the pickup which had a canopy; one child was in the cab; two others slept in Dad's car; and Maxine & I were in a small tent. The air mattresses went flat, so we were there wishing for daylight when a bear came along and began making a racket with our clean pans on the table.

"Oh, oh! A bear!" Mom exclaimed, awakened by the noise. I yelled at the bear and he left. We all got up then, though it was only 4:30AM. We fixed ham and eggs for breakfast–maybe hotcakes, too. It was so cold that when the grease ran over the griddle and down on the edge of the stove it congealed to form a stalagmite. After this hasty breakfast the folks headed north for home, while we went back down to work in Yosemite Valley.

Final Preparations

At last the time had come for final preparations for overseas service. The General Missionary Board (now Free Methodist World Missions) was ready to send us to Greenville Hospital in South Africa. In anticipation of this we sent them our passports and other documents in order to get visas for this assignment. However, in early October Personnel Director Don Bowen called me asking if we would be willing to go to Burundi instead, as Dr. Ensign needed to come home. (His son Scott was having serious medical problems).

"That's fine with us," I replied. "The only snag is that Burundi requires doctors to have a tropical medicine course and this is October. I'm sure the courses in both Liverpool, England and Tulane University (New Orleans, Louisiana) have already started."

"Yes, we realize that," Dr. Bowen said, "So I have contacted Tulane University, and they will accept you in the second half of their course. They can give you a certificate of tropical medicine that will be accepted by the Burundi government."

"These plans sound good to us," I replied. We were happy to be assigned to the mountains of Central Africa where Kibuye Hospital was awaiting our help. We'd been singing the old Gospel song *"I'll go where you want me to go dear Lord"* by changing the last words to *"dear Board"*. The General Missionary Board's first idea had been to send our family to India, then to South Africa, and now finally to Burundi. We believed the Lord was guiding us through the mission board. Central Africa had actually been our first choice of location.

My next thought was *what shall I do from late October until January 1970 when we go to New Orleans?* I called down to Modesto to Scenic General and asked the director of medical education if I might come and be a staff physician for those few months. She agreed, so we moved back to Modesto and experienced God's provision in a marvelous way.

We had sold our house in Modesto, intending to leave for South Africa following the summer at Yosemite. But now, here we were, with new plans and needing to stay in Modesto several more months. Al Flory, a builder in our Modesto FM Church, had a new house built that he had not yet sold. He gave us the keys at no cost to us, and with furnishings on loan from other church members, we moved in for two months.

Another provision of God was being put on the gynecology service at Scenic General. This meant I was able to learn several more difficult procedures in that department which stood me in good stead later in missionary service when I was the only surgeon.

Then it was on to Louisiana where I received good training in tropical diseases at Tulane. We left New Orleans in May of 1970, driving to Chicago where we sold our '65 Dodge to other missionary friends. We boarded a plane to Addis Abba, Ethiopia, as the first leg of our journey to Burundi. A highlight of our stopover in Addis was visiting a Baptist hospital near the city.

When we went to the airport several days later to catch our ongoing flight to Nairobi, Kenya we found that our plane had left eight hours early because of work on the runway! Of course, they had no way of notifying us of this change. Fortunately, some kind missionaries took care of us for three more days before we could get another flight to Bujumbura. Our colleagues in Burundi had no idea why we had not arrived as planned, and were relieved when we finally showed up safe and sound at the Bujumbura International Airport, our final destination.

More preparation in Burundi

We took in our new surroundings–a hot and humid city whose streets were filled with vehicles and pedestrians. It is situated on Lake Tanganyika, longest lake in Africa at 2,500 feet of elevation. We saw mountains rising up from the city to well over 7,000 feet, covered with lush vegetation, primarily eucalyptus and banana trees. Later, we would drive up and over these mountains, putting on a sweater as the temperature went down, and seeing different trees, mainly Arusha pines. Our destination was Kibuye Mission Station, 100 miles away.

Before making that journey; however, I was required to have a short internship, called in French, a *stage* (pronounced *stahge*). This was done in a government hospital in Bujumbura in order to be certified to practice medicine in Burundi. During this time I did a lot of surgery and my supervisors liked my skill so well they made me extend my six-week *stage* to eight.

Dr. Merton Alexander had been filling in as the only doctor at Kibuye Hospital. After I arrived he moved to our sister hospital at Kibogora in neighboring Rwanda. With my *stage* behind me I was ready to tackle the medical work. However, the matter of local language acquisition was still before me. Kirundi is a pretty difficult language and I was grateful to have Betty Ellen Cox, our resident linguist, for a teacher. For the first six months I worked mornings at the hospital and studied Kirundi with her in the afternoons. Even so, after all these years, I have never gained real fluency in Kirundi.

Old Kibuye Hospital, 1971

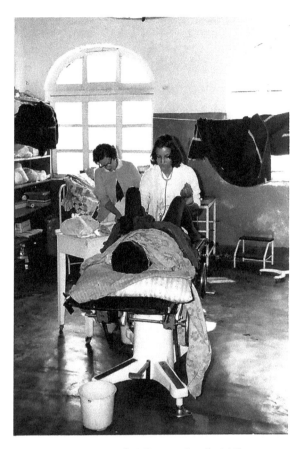

Nurses Doris Moore & Minerva Snell at Kibuye, 1971

When making rounds in the hospital wards, I would talk to the patients in Kirundi, phrasing my questions so that the answers would be a simple yes or no, but it didn't always work well. As soon as patients heard me speaking Kirundi they would start jabbering away, giving their whole medical history, and I rarely understood fully. It could be a big problem if I got it wrong, and a mistake in my profession could be fatal. I would turn to my accompanying nurse and get a translation into French. I am much better in French. In the operating room it was even better for me because I had staff that were also good in English.

Maxine took Kirundi lessons with Betty Ellen, too, but she had the added challenge of running a home in rural Africa with a busy husband and three children. We employed domestic help and outside workers as was the custom, both to give employment to local people, and due to all the labor involved in everyday survival.

For example, if she wanted spaghetti for dinner she began by sending a worker to look for ripe tomatoes in the garden or in the market, then she made the sauce from scratch. If she wanted salad or a cooked vegetable it depended on what was ripe in the garden. Maxine made her own mayonnaise and salad dressings. Since bread was not available in those early years we enjoyed home-baked bread and rolls made by Maxine or our cook, Eugene Bigirimana (who was later killed in the civil war). Ezechiel Bucumi worked for us after that. These men learned to cook all our favorite recipes as Maxine translated them into Kirundi. Groceries that we *could* buy were limited and many miles away.

For schooling, the two boys attended a small boarding school for MK's (missionary kids) at Mweya some 20 miles away. They were only permitted to go home one 3-day weekend a month, which was hard on us as parents. Little sister Ronda also missed her brothers. However, she had Mama's full attention at home for pre-school and kindergarten. Maxine also cared for abandoned babies; sewed surgical drapes and gowns for the hospital; and looked after mission accounts.

Wes & Ronda Ogden having fun with barrels from USA, 1971

Witch Doctors

In those early years we had some trouble with witch doctors. One week I had operated on three men with stomach ulcers. They were doing well postoperatively but in the morning I found them all dead. Then I learned that some witch doctors had come in the night and given them medicines that killed them. *Were they doing this to spite me for my "scientific" medicine? Were they thinking their medicine would help in recovery*? I'll never know; however, because of that, the hospital census dropped to three for a time. It didn't help that a rumor was being circulated that I operated in order to get choice pieces of meat to eat. We were able to work through that and eventually regain the respect of the population.

Most unusual case

"I've been pregnant for eighteen months," announced a lady who came to the hospital one day. Of course I scoffed at that impossibility. In those years I did not have an ultrasound machine, but when I examined this woman I found that she had a large mass in the lower abdomen. When I operated, I found there was, indeed, a baby inside, but it was not alive.

This is what happened: At nine months the mother had gone into labor and headed toward the hospital. Before she got there the contractions stopped, so she turned around and went home, not realizing that the uterus had ruptured, sending the baby and placenta into the abdominal cavity. The uterus was able to contract down, and she did not bleed to death as she should have. The body had built a membrane around the "tumor" which protected the mother from infection. She waited another nine months before coming to see me. I removed the dead baby and she did very well after that.

BIG KNIFE "Kibugita"

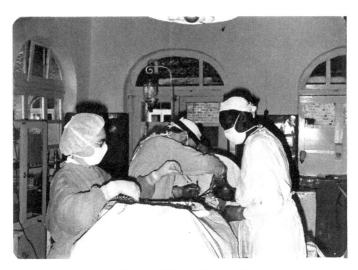

Operating at Kibuye Hospital, 1976

Bill, Maxine, Ronda, Frank, Wes Ogden
at Kumbya Retreat Center, Rwanda, 1977

Fleas

One of the trials I faced was a tiny bug that caused a persistent problem. When I went to work, I would often get flea bites because patients brought fleas to the hospital. It was difficult to be itching and to scratch the many flea bites. In fact, it's impossible to get relief when gowned up for surgery. I got the idea that wearing a flea collar for dogs around each ankle might be helpful. I obtained small flea collars from the US and put one around each ankle over my sock. I didn't have to scratch any longer. Fleas quit attacking me. Then I discovered that just one was effective. Soon after this I was sitting in the living room of Bishop Aaron Ruhumuriza in Kigali, when a retired missionary, Burton McCready, was visiting. He was really tickled to see that I was wearing a flea collar on my ankle.

Typhus

Epidemic typhus is a rickettsia disease. Rickettsia are similar but are not bacteria nor viruses. In Burundi in the early 1970's epidemic, louse borne typhus was rampant throughout the country. At first I took a team of workers to distribute small pouches of DDT in the communities to kill the lice, but this had limited or no success. Later it became known throughout the world to be harmful to birds and perhaps humans, so DDT is not used anymore as a pesticide.

As the epidemic continued the hospital filled up with patients having high fevers (over 40 degrees C) and mortality near one hundred percent. *What could I do about this?* I learned that doxycycline (Vibramycin) had effect against this rickettsia, and the maker of Vibramycin, Pfizer Laboratory, wanted me to do a clinical trial. I agreed, and they gave us the Vibramycin 100mg capsules. Our study soon showed that *a single capsule* of Vibramycin changed the mortality from one hundred percent, to *zero*.

Finding this remarkable Pfizer asked me to present my findings at the International Conference on Chemotherapy in Prague, Czechoslovakia the next year.

"I can't go to that conference unless I spend some time at a medical library to become more of an expert on this disease. Nairobi, Kenya is the nearest medical library," I said.

"Fine!" They replied. "Take the family to Kenya. We will pay everything." And so, the five of us flew to Nairobi and Pfizer put is in the five star Norfolk Hotel very close to the university where the medical library is located.

I returned to Burundi for more research, then some three months later I mentioned that I needed to return to the library again. Once more Pfizer agreed, sending the entire family to Nairobi again, this time putting us in the Hilton, and later during our stay, the Intercontinental Hotel. I was finally able to finish the draft of my presentation for the conference in Prague.

I flew to Prague without the family, a long trip involving two flights. When I finally arrived at the hotel in Prague I was having a headache. *O my, I must be getting malaria and I left my prophylaxis medicine at home in Burundi!* A doctor from New York who was also attending the conference the next day insisted that we get help and spoke to the hotel clerk about it. Soon an ambulance arrived, and with her English explained my problem. The ambulance took me to the First Aid Station where I sat on a bench not knowing what was to happen. I had no Czech language and my few words of German were not helpful, so I just sat.

Soon another ambulance came and took me to the infectious disease hospital where I was admitted and examined by a Russian lady doctor who spoke some English. I explained my allergy to chloroquine, the usual treatment for malaria at that time.

"What I need is Paludrine," I told her. That made sense to her and she went away I was then put into a terrible, hard rack resembling a bed, and I waited. At about 10:00 PM a nurse came and handed me a little envelope containing some pills. She gave me no water or anything else with which to swallow the pills.

I had taken Tylenol before I left the hotel so my headache was gone. I didn't have malaria after all, and now I had in my hand what I needed for prophylaxis; *but* here I was stuck in this hospital on this uncomfortable bed, scheduled to present an important paper at a big meeting in the morning. *What am I going to do?*

About this time a more senior doctor came to my room. We were able to communicate in French. I explained my situation to him. I asked for a taxi back to the hotel.

"There are no taxis in Prague at this hour of the night," he said. (After all, we were in Communist Europe.) *Oh no, I wonder what I can I do?* He mumbled something more and left. He soon returned, motioning me to follow, and placed me in a third ambulance. This one returned me to the hotel. All of this cost me nothing. I was able to make my presentation the next day. At the conclusion of the conference the moderator said that two of the presentations had special merit and mine was one of them.

We have used Vibramycin since that time, and epidemic typhus has been eradicated from Burundi. I have not seen it for years.

Orthopedic Cases

When telling American congregations about my orthopedic cases I always began with this one: I had a Volvo car at Kibuye that had many holes in the exhaust pipe. I was unable to get a replacement, so I went to the hospital, got some casting plaster, crawled under the car and applied a cast to the pipe. That helped for quite a while until rain gradually ruined it. Too bad I didn't have the fiberglass casting material now used.

Many unusual situations occur when you are the only doctor, and especially a surgeon, in Central Africa. Some patients come with chronic osteo-myelitis, an infection in the bone, most frequently in a leg. They present with a very swollen leg, draining pus from the wound. These are not amenable to cure with antibiotics because they have within the infection some dead bone & other necrotic material. This must be removed surgically, and in order for it to heal, the wound is left open. This takes prolonged healing time and sometimes skin grafts are needed for final closure.

These patients are often kept in bed for weeks to months, with dressing changes every day. Often I would need to use pain medicine or even anesthesia for the painful dressing change. In the US most osteo-myelitis is caught in the acute phase and treated with antibiotics, not needing surgical intervention. Interestingly, Mickey Mantle had this disease.

One day we sat calmly having our meal in our Kibuye home when suddenly we heard a loud crash across the valley. Rushing down with our van we found that a Toyota taxi-van had rolled over down the forty-foot embankment. Eight injured passengers were transported the short distance to the hospital. The most critically injured was a twenty year-old man. He was confused and delirious. He had multiply abrasions and bilateral fractures of the femurs (both thigh bones were broken). He was in no condition for operative repair of the femur fractures, so we placed pins in the legs just below the knees and put him in traction to reduce the fractures.

Usually it takes eight to ten weeks for bone to grow while in traction; then you get the patient up to walk using the good leg for support; but this young man did not have a leg to stand on. Thus, it was necessary to discontinue the traction but to keep him in bed for six months for the new bone to be strong enough to support his weight.

If you or I were kept in bed for six months, I think we would be sad and discouraged. However, when I made ward rounds, I found this patient quite cheerful. He had gladly received the other treatment all our patients are offered—the Good News about forgiveness of sins through Jesus Christ. This young man had become a Christian during his hospital stay, and his countenance showed that change. After six months we walked him in parallel bars; then crutches; then sent him home. Four months later he returned to give us back the crutches, and he was still showing the love of God. We had given him more than just good medical care.

Reconnaissance

In 1971 I was asked to accompany Gerald Bates, (then Africa Area Assistant to the Director of Free Methodist World Missions) to Nundu, Zaire (now DRC) to explore the possibility of establishing a hospital there. We found a small church, a lot of grass three feet high and the ruins of residences left by British Pentecostal missionaries.

We made our report to The Free Methodist Church of Zaire and the mission leaders in Indiana. They went ahead with plans to open a hospital by sending Jim & Barb Stillman, Al & Helen Nelson and Myra Adamson. Al was a pastor & builder; Jim a jack of all trades; Barb and Myra nurses; and Helen facilitated, fed and worked with finances.

Building teams came from North America to assist. Soon a small clinic was opened while Al began building the hospital. I returned later when this was in process and actually performed an operation on an ordinary table in this clinic with Myra's help. There wasn't even a screen on the window. Today, there is a thriving church, hospital and nurses training school, staffed entirely by Africans. (See congohealth.org)

Civil War and Two Rescues

It was 1972 and we were in our second year of service. Politically, things were getting very difficult in Burundi. An uprising to unseat the Tutsi government had failed and reprisals (genocide against the majority tribe of Hutus) ensued with killing by the military of over 250,000 Hutus, especially any with education. We missionaries were not targeted, but it was difficult to work and very tense in the country.

At least one missionary was imprisoned for a short time and banished from the country with just 24 hours to leave. He left his family behind to follow later. Many of our African friends were killed around us. Gunfire was often heard. Travel was quite restricted, but as a doctor I was given permission to do so. Maxine and I took our three children up to Kibogora mission station in Rwanda to stay with friends rather than be subjected to all the sound of gunfire and other tensions, and we returned to work at Kibuye.

We knew that the soldiers were looking for one of our lab nurses, Francois Ncishako, and he asked if we could help him flee to Tanzania. Since the mission had a double-cab VW pickup with a luggage compartment under the back seat large enough for a man to lie inside, I agreed.

"Put Francois in that compartment before daylight," I told Zacharie Kazungu, mission station manager, *so I would not see him and therefore could truthfully answer any soldier who might stop to ask me questions.* "I will get him near the Tanzania border."

Early the next morning I got in the truck and drove to Buhonga near the Tanzania border where my "hidden cargo" was able to walk to the river which was the international border. Francois got in a dugout canoe and started paddling across the river. When gunshots rang out he jumped into the water and swam to safety. (Some years later Francois returned to Kibuye to continue working as a nurse. This is when I learned about his narrow escape after I had left him at the border.)

After that I drove on to Kayero to check on three single missionary ladies who had no permission to travel, essentially "stuck" on their mission compound. They told me the generator of their hydro was broken down and the batteries nearly dead, which meant their shortwave radio was out. (Remember, this was long before cell phones.) I was able to find some emery cloth and fix the commutator of the generator attached to the water wheel of the hydro, so they would have lights and radio contact with the outside world.

I drove on home by nightfall. In these times of civil war in Africa, control is maintained by setting up roadblocks or checkpoints every few miles. That day I passed through a total of ten checkpoints. When I reached the last checkpoint right by the gate to the mission the soldiers hassled me. That was the last straw. I had really *had it* by then. We also realized it was not good for our small children to know that their parents were in a war zone. Maxine and I packed up our little VW Variant that night; said goodbye to Doris Moore and other staff; and left the next day for Kibogora to rejoin our sons and daughter. Our journey would take us first to Bujumbura, with the plan of driving on to Kibogora the next day.

In the meantime, David Riley of the Friends Mission, who had heard how I had taken Francois to safety in Tanzania, learned of our plan to leave the next day for Rwanda. He had an older model of the same type of VW double-cab pickup with the large compartment under the back seat. David came to see me.

"Our worker at CORDAC Christian Radio, B.T (name has been changed), is being hunted (because he was an educated Hutu)." I have this old pickup like your later model VW. I don't care if I never get it back. Will you drive it out of the country with B.T. under the back seat for us?"

"Yes, I will do it," I said. "Put him under the back seat before daylight tomorrow, and I will drive him to safety. Of course, you will all be praying." It went without saying that if he were discovered at a check-point it would not go well for him or me.

We did this as planned, and Maxine followed in our VW Variant. I put a case of 24 bottles of Coke on that seat. We went through seven checkpoints, including the international border with Zaire (DRC) and B.T. did not cough or sneeze and was not discovered. We breathed a big sigh of relief and gave thanks to God.

We stopped and got B.T. out from under the seat once we were safely in Zaire. I offered him a Coke, but he was so emotionally tied up inside that he declined, though he had been in there more than four hours. Later he was able to drink a coke and we drove on to Kibogora. (One route from Bujumbura, Burundi to

Kibogora, Rwanda, passes through a corner of Zaire. This got us out of Burundi faster).

B.T.'s family was able to join him later. His wife merely carried her smallest child on her back in the Congolese fashion and walked across at the border post. Pastor B.T. then became a faithful leader in the Rwanda Free Methodist Church, serving at different times as pastor, superintendent and chaplain at Kibogora Hospital.

In 1994 this faithful servant had to flee once more when things became difficult in Rwanda. The Tutsi rebels took over the government and many Hutu leaders fled to neighboring Congo. B.T. & his family were among these refugees. In exile there he served the church for three years. I saw him when he returned to Kibogora in 1997, very undernourished from living off roots in the forest but still full of faith. I offered him my extra shoes. He said, *"Thank you, thank you! Now I can give my wife back her sandals."*

Pastor B.T. continues to be one of the reasons that we returned again and again to help our friends who are pointing others to our Lord and Savior Jesus Christ. We serve a wonderful God who cares for His own.

Interesting update: In Feb. 2018, in our retirement, we received a letter from B.T. in which he was thanking God for all His mercies throughout his life, and thanking the Free Methodist Church in Rwanda, Burundi and Congo, plus all the missionaries who helped him, including us. He said in that letter "I am 74 years old. Please pray for me as I want to serve God right up to the day I'll die."

Chapter 5

TRAVEL ADVENTURES

B ack to 1972… At Kibogora we were reunited with our children and decided we should return to the States. For one thing Dr. Al Snyder, a general surgeon, was now there so I wasn't needed as much. For another, Maxine was not doing well with the happenings in Burundi—constant tension and news of death all around us. In God's Providence, we got word from Dr. Ben Burgoyne of an opportunity to practice medicine and surgery in Arlington, Washington.

Moving to Arlington

One of the perks of living overseas is the possibility of planning family vacations in foreign countries both going to Africa and returning to the States. These were educational times for our children and a good way to unwind from the stresses of everyday life. So on this trip back to the States we flew to Geneva, Switzerland and on to Copenhagen, Denmark. Our boys caused some amusing looks in the airports as they carried their suitcases on their heads. They had learned from Africans that carrying a load on your head can save the strain on your shoulders and back. After all, these were the days before there were wheels on our bags.

At the airport in Copenhagen Bill was looking at an SAS timetable.

"Dad!" he said, "They have a direct flight to Seattle. Let's get on it!" He had had enough travel by now through Africa and Europe and wanted to get home to the US. I told him that we had to go first to Winona Lake, Indiana to report to our boss at the World Missions office.

When we finally got home to Washington State we went to Arlington where I entered into practice with Dr. Norm Zook and Dr. Ben Burgoyne. We made plans for each of us to go in turn for a year of missionary service while the others supported him from home. They each spent a year at Greenville Hospital in South Africa.

It was during our time at Arlington that we bought a cabin at Lake Cavanaugh. On a beautiful Sunday afternoon in 1975 we took a drive to Lake Cavanaugh, 20 miles from home, on mostly gravel roads. A For Sale by Owner sign on a cabin looked interesting, so we returned home and called the owner. We were shown the unfinished cabin and bought it for $21,500. It had no running water or septic system, but it did have an outhouse, and we carried water in buckets from the lake. This was fine for our occasional weekend get-away. Little did we know, this cabin, as it was developed over time, would become our main residence in the United States.

Besides getting involved in a busy medical clinic we were active in starting the Arlington Christian School. When our boys were beyond the level of instruction there we formed a car pool so they could drive to King's Garden School (now Kings High) in Shoreline. Bill drove our nine-passenger Dodge Van most of the time, though the driving was sometimes shared.

Returning to Africa—the long way

After four years in Arlington it was time to return to Africa. I left the medical practice in Washington to the care of another doctor. It was now the summer of 1976. Maxine and I made preparations for our second missionary journey, taking only the two younger children this time: 15-year old Wes & 10-year old Ronda. Bill had decided to finish his senior year of high school at Kings, staying with Uncle Jerry & Aunt Laverne Reed in Lynnwood.

We were headed back to Burundi to serve once again at Kibuye Hospital. An added bonus— My parents, Rev. H. W. & Wilma Ogden would later join us there. (By now, my Dad had retired as a pastor and Army Chaplain). He was a big help with the construction of our new hospital facility, and also ministered in our Free Methodist Churches. Mother became a home-school teacher for Wes & Ronda.

This time we chose to fly west to Africa, making stops in Manila (to visit missionary friends), Iran, and then a week in the Holy Land. These were wonderful experiences for our family. The most meaningful part of the trip for me was visiting the Garden Tomb where we could see where Jesus' body was placed after the crucifixion.

You cannot touch where the body had lain, but when you turn around inside the tomb you see above the door a sign which says, *"He is not here, He is risen."* The message is clear—we serve a Risen Savior. Emerging from the tomb we took Communion in the garden, reflecting on this wonderful foundation of our faith. From the Garden Tomb we could see the hill of Golgotha, not far away.

When the travel agent at the hotel in Jerusalem checked our ongoing tickets to Nairobi, Kenya, he said, "There's no flight that day as it's a Jewish holiday, but we can route you through Athens to Bujumbura, Burundi." Once in Athens, we checked in with Sabena Airlines for our flight that evening to Bujumbura and were told, "We are not going to Bujumbura tonight. There's been a coup d'etat in Burundi today." We had come more than halfway around the world to be told that we could not return to Burundi which we had left four years earlier in a time of war.

Maxine said, "Let's get the next plane to New York." I had another idea. "We can take that same flight we are booked on and just get off when they make their stop in Kigali, Rwanda, then fly to Kamembe and drive to our mission hospital at Kibogora." The airline agent said, "No, we cannot board passengers who do not have a visa for their destination." Oh, I thought about that for a minute.

I knew that the small country of Rwanda would not have an embassy in Athens, so I asked, "Where is the Zaire Embassy?" She said, "Forty-five minutes across the city by taxi, and it closes in one hour." We grabbed a taxi; got to the embassy; filled out the papers; and got the visas. The ambassador signed our passports and left for the day before we even finished the applications.

My thought was that we could get off the flight in Kigali, take the small plane across Rwanda to the border town of Kamembe, then cross the river-border into Zaire. Our missionary friends, Gerald & Marlene

Bates, who lived in the border town of Bukavu, could put us up until things were calm in Burundi. From there we could drive to Kibuye. Sometimes in missionary life, you have to make adjustments and alternate plans.

We flew all night to Kigali and landed OK, only to be told, "There is no fuel for the plane to Kamembe, and so we will transport you by taxi-van to Cyangugu (near Kamembe)." This was an all-day trip on rough dirt roads, twisting through the mountains of the Nyungwe Forest in Rwanda. All this after flying all night from Athens. We were very tired by the time we reached the Sabena Airlines agent in Cyangugu. He tried by radio and telephone to contact Gerald Bates across the river but was unsuccessful. He said, "Even though they aren't home you must get across the river now because the border closes at 6:00 PM."

So with our two children and all our luggage for missionary service, Maxine and I boarded a small raft which was propelled hand over hand on a cable across the Ruzizi River. And that's how we entered Zaire. The crossing was fine, but now the soldiers informed us that the border was closed. They kindly offered to keep our luggage & passports while we went into town for the night. I replied, "No way are we leaving our luggage." We knew from previous experience that many things could "disappear" from unattended luggage.

By now it was getting dark and we had no vehicle. In God's provision, a kind Indian man was at the border post and gave us a lift to the Bates' house, only a few miles away Amazingly, Gerald and Marlene had returned home just five minutes before. (Incidentally, we did leave our passports with the border agents,

53

knowing we would retrieve them the following day when the officials would be on duty to stamp us into the country).

After resting for a week from our long, adventurous trip to Africa Gerald drove us to Bujumbura. As it turned out, the coup d'état was a minor one, to change a president who was not governing well. Only a few, if any, had died in the takeover. *Thus* began our second term of service at Kibuye Hospital for nearly two years.

Back to Arlington via new countries

In April, 1978 it was time to return to Arlington for my rotation with the doctors there. In order to see more of the world we flew to Nairobi, Kenya; Johannesburg and Cape Town, South Africa; and across the Atlantic Ocean to Rio de Janeiro, Brazil. We visited missionary friends in Sao Paolo and made a brief stop at Iguassu Falls, which is one of the greatest falls in the world. Our plane circled right over it before landing. Argentina and Paraguay also come together at Iguassu Falls, so we walked over into Argentina a short way. The next stop was Asuncion, Paraguay to visit missionary friends, Ernie and Lucy Houston. For our ongoing flight to Lima, Peru, we had to wait four hours while an engine on our Lockheed Electra plane was fixed. This delay meant that we flew over the Andes at night.

During the flight I noticed a bright light being shone on that repaired engine. Being a pilot, I wished I could see the instruments to know the exhaust gas temperature. I knew we could fly the Andes on just three engines but if it caught fire, that would be a different story. Our big four-engine turbo-prop plane made the trip fine. We made a short visit to Inca Ruins nearby.

On we flew to Mexico City, Los Angeles and Seattle. We had planned our trip to be home in April in time to see Bill in the all-school play at King's High School. However, he hadn't told us what part he was playing, so imagine our surprise when the curtain went up and there was Bill as the star in "A Man Called Peter". He had developed the Scottish brogue of Peter Marshall and never missed a line of that great play.

We came home to Arlington, to the same house that we had in 1975, and I worked in the same medical practice for six months. Then we moved to Centralia, Washington to join Dr. David Williams in practice. We had a five-acre place where we kept two horses and three steers, convenient to town and work. One time I needed air in the tractor tires, so I drove it to town instead of the car, stopping to make rounds on my patients in the hospital. I got some strange looks as I pulled in to the doctors' parking area,

Chapter 6

MEDICAL CHALLENGES

W e often had more surgical cases than we were able to handle because our old sterilizer was so slow that we couldn't get instruments and surgical drapes ready in time. This meant holding patients over for surgery until the next day. For example, one day at Kibogora I did a thyroidectomy, a hysterectomy and a repair of a patellar tendon (knee). A fourth case, a hernia, had to be re-scheduled. It's hard to tell someone who has fasted all day that we cannot operate until tomorrow. He could go ahead and eat that evening but must fast again tomorrow until his operation.

Another time things got very hectic at Kibogora. I ran out of materials so held over one patient for surgery the next day. But then I fell ill, so I wasn't much good the next day. However, I got up and did ten gastroscopies (see next section on Peptic Ulcer Disease), then went back to bed. Dr. Paul Yardy was covering for me, but a lady was brought in with a ruptured uterus, so I went down and we did a Cesarean hysterectomy to save her life. Of course, the baby didn't make it. We finished that operation at 11:00 PM, and I was just able to drag myself up the hill and to bed. (In all my years in surgery I have only been able to save two babies from ruptured uterus, and that was because the rupture occurred while we had her on the table getting prepped to operate.)

FO & Dr. Al Snyder, Kibogora,   FO with Drs. Beata & Georges,
late 1970's   Kibogora,1998

During my time at Kibogora I would make ten-day visits to Nundu. I would usually do seven operations per day, if I could get enough time and materials to do them. There was no air-conditioning, so it was difficult to be gowned & gloved with temps and humidity in the nineties. I had a little 12-volt truck fan but needed a lot more moving air.

A sample case from these days was a man brought in from a bicycle accident with open fracture of both leg bones (tibia & fibula). There was not much grass and dirt in the wounds, so we cleaned them out carefully, sutured them closed and applied a plaster splint. Often when wounds such as this have much contamination, we do not close the wounds until sometime later.

During rainy season a deluge of rain could flood our homes or hospital buildings, such as the time we had water running under the door of the operating room. I had to get it cleaned up before I could operate.

Much of the time in Africa I worked without any blood bank. We did see ruptured splecns, lacerated livers, and gastrointestinal bleeding which we were able to treat successfully. We got the patient out of shock with IV fluids and rapid surgical intervention to stop the internal bleeding. Then we let them build their blood back up with iron therapy.

Sometimes we were able to crossmatch and give proper blood, for example, from the family member who brought the patient to the hospital. A couple of times we got type O blood from a missionary, which can be used in emergency for *any* patient, to save his life.

We were very thankful when the Rwandan government brought electricity (hydro-electric power) to Kibogora in 1984, and to Kibuye in 2001. Until then we had to do everything with kerosene lamps or diesel generator. However, in the Operating Room I had 12-Volt lights from the solar panels I had installed. In our homes we had kerosene refrigerators which worked well except they were fussy to keep going. Thus we didn't have one at the hospital because it might not be watched carefully in the night. That's when Maxine had to accommodate blood along with our personal food and drinks in our home fridge.

Many patients came with late presentation of malignant tumors. Some were beyond any help apart from telling them about Christ so they could prepare to die. Others were operated, hoping for a cure, though odds were not good. Nevertheless, many received palliation to have useful living for months or sometimes years.

One example is when a young lady came to Kibogora with a really extensive face tumor that was pushing her nose to the left. For better anesthesia we took her to the nearest hospital that could give the right kind of anesthesia necessary for this operation. The operation went well. The post-operative photo shows her much improved and after the swelling went down it was even better. Although she did well and I hoped for a full cure she was lost to follow-up, as is so often the case in Africa.

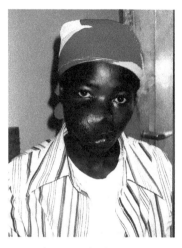 

Facial cancer before surgery   Facial cancer after surgery

A man came with a very large tumor of the lower jaw. I was glad to have the help of Dr. Wayne Dickason, a plastic surgeon friend visiting from Olympia, Washington. This was a complex case because it required removal of a large portion of the patient's mandible. Then we repaired the defect by taking a pedicle graft from his rib, complete with muscle, skin and vascular supply. We swung it up under the clavicle to rebuild his jaw. This made a remarkable improvement and no doubt saved his life. We also told him about eternal life with Christ, as all our patients get visited by the chaplain during their stay in the hospital.

BIG KNIFE "Kibugita"

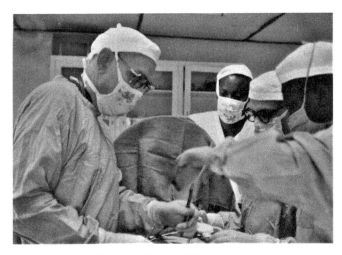

FO operating at Kibuye, 1990

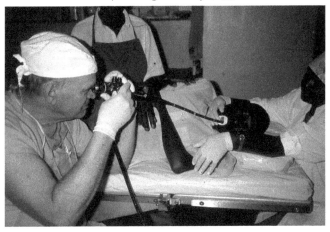

Endoscopy for peptic ulcers

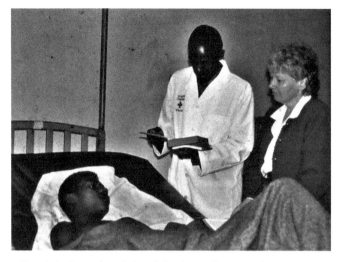

Chaplain Pascal and Carol Ogden talking with patient at Kibuye (courtesy of F.E. Walls)

"Get back here. That man will eat you!" I overheard a mother telling her child. We were shopping at an open air market in Rwanda. In the early years it was rumored that white people ate little children.

"O, don't worry! I like children, but not to eat them." I answered in Kinyarwanda (language of Rwanda). You should have seen her face. She had no idea that I understood her language. Superstitions in the culture like this were sometimes an obstacle.

One time a ten-year old boy was brought to Kibuye with an entero-cutaneus fistula, an abnormal channel from the small intestine to the skin on the abdomen. I don't know the actual cause but I believe it was some type of injury. He came with a large area of skin and abdominal wall missing, with discharge of liquid which was partially digested food. As you can imagine, this boy had become very malnourished because most of what he ate was lost.

We tried to get it cleaned up in order to get it closed, but I had to leave without accomplishing that. Nurses changed dressings twice a day. We did not have available TPN (Total Parenteral Nutrition). That is where high-protein, fat, and other nutrients are given intravenously, while withholding all oral intake. One might even have a nasogastric tube in the stomach to suck out acid and other gastric juices. But we had none of that and there was nothing else we could do. I felt that he was near death.

Nearly a year later my nurses brought to me a very well-nourished boy, grinning from ear to ear "Doctor, do you remember this boy as a patient?"

"No I don't recognize him." I said.

"He's the boy that nearly died with the big cutaneous drainage from his abdomen."

"Oh! I thought that he had surely died. This is a miracle of healing. Praise God!"

I like the Kirundi for "Praise God," *Imana ishimwe,* which is used a lot as we have seen God working when our efforts at healing are inadequate; either due to lack of materials or training, or simply that the situation is beyond medical science. *Igitangaza* is another great Kirundi word meaning "miracle". I would hear this word around the hospital, too, as we medical personnel realized that God is working with us in the healing of both the body and soul.

Peptic Ulcer Disease

The Burundian people have a high incidence of peptic ulcer disease, so I was called upon to do a lot of gastric surgery. In fact, one year, out of the 800 major operations I performed, 400 were for these ulcers. Word got around that I could cure people of this problem and I soon became known as the doctor who operated on stomachs. Patients with peptic ulcers would come from far and wide to be cared for at Kibuye Hospital.

Usually these patients are adults who have suffered with the disease for many years. However, once I saw a seven-year old with gastric outlet obstruction due to peptic ulcer. He was just skin and bones so we called him the Matchstick Kid. His extremities were extremely emaciated. We were able to operate on him successfully. When I saw him months later I did not recognize him at all.

"That's the Matchstick Kid," one of my staff said. "Look how much he has grown!" This was encouraging as we don't often see the patients who have done well.

To determine if a person has a peptic ulcer, the first step is to look into the stomach with a long rubber tube which has a fiber optic core (gastroscope). This allowed me to look directly at the ulcers in the stomach or the duodenum (the first part of the small intestine). Often, I saw a lot of scarring from so much acid. This acted as an obstruction so the food couldn't pass through. Many people had suffered with the disease for 20 years or more before they came to the hospital.

To treat peptic ulcer disease with medicines was usually not a good solution for me since we couldn't get all the fancy medicines available in North America. Also, the patients couldn't afford those medicines even if we had them. So I operated on these cases, doing a vagotomy and gastrojejunostomy, or occasionally a hemigastrectomy. This meant cutting the vagus nerve which shuts off acid production in the stomach, diverting the food to the 2nd part of the small intestine. This "bypass" surgery gives 99 percent cure rate, and it only cost $15 (at the time I was there). That was a little cheaper than in the US!

I'm often asked "Why are there so many peptic ulcers?" There are mainly three reasons that ethnic Hutu and Tutsi people (that is, Burundians, Rwandans and the Tutsis living in the highlands of Congo) have such a tendency to have peptic ulcers. The primary cause is being taught from infancy to never show their emotions; to turn their fear and anger inwards. They say nothing; they just stew inside, producing acid in the stomach that eats a hole in the duodenum (first part of the small intestine).

Another contributing factor is that these tribal groups drink large amounts of beer from the local brewery, or the homemade kind made from bananas or sorghum.

A third cause for so much peptic ulcer disease is the *helicobacter pylori* bacteria which is present in their countries just as it is in ours. I noticed that other African tribes (non-Hutu or Tutsi), though they drink the same beers and are exposed to the same bacteria, rarely get the ulcer disease. Why? Because they are not stoic, and freely let out their emotions.

Since I had operated on so many people for peptic ulcers and since Burundi is a small country, we sometimes ran into these cured patients later. Everyone knew we were there in Burundi to help and we had a large sign we could put in the front window of our hospital van that announced "Kibuye Hospital". This identified us when rolling up to roadblocks or border crossings, especially during the war years. One day we were driving up the main street of Bujumbura, our sign prominently displayed, and we noticed a pick-up truck ahead of us with people standing in the back, facing our direction. This is a typical means of transport. Suddenly, to our amazement and amusement, a man pulled up his shirt and pointed to his abdominal scar, a big grin on his face. It could only mean one thing: I had operated on him for peptic ulcer disease.

At border crossings into Rwanda or returning to Burundi the agents have recognized me, which helped to expedite sometimes lengthy waits in crossing the international borders. For example, one officer was slowly going through a pile of passports. It looked like we would be there for a long time. Then he came to ours and looked up.

"Oh, Dr. Ogden! You're the one who operated on my father! He is doing so well now." This was followed by a quick stamp in our passports and we were on our way.

Unusual Cases

A seven-year old girl was brought in who had been vomiting for three months. She was just skin and bones, so not a good surgical candidate; but if we did not operate she would soon die. It turned out that she had a mal-rotation of the intestine, resulting in fibrous bands blocking the small bowel. She was born this way so it's a wonder she reached age seven before coming to us. We divided the bands to relieve the obstruction. We also did an appendectomy, since her appendix was on the left side (not the usual right side), which would make it difficult to diagnosis appendicitis if she ever got it later in life. She did very well and went home happy.

More than once a small boy was brought by a parent with a bean stuck in his ear. I got used to seeing that, but the time I pulled out a ball bearing was a bit unusual.

I wasn't always operating on Africans in Africa. North American missionaries, aid workers from various agencies, Chinese laborers from the cement plant and Peace Corps people also came to our hospitals. One of these particular cases involved missionary Dorothy Orcutt, who was at that time the head nurse at Kibogora. She was nearing retirement but chose to have her operation in Rwanda before returning to the States.

Maxine and I were living at Kibuye at the time when Dorothy's hysterectomy was scheduled. Dr. Al Snyder asked me by radio—during one of our regular contacts between mission stations–if I would come to assist him. I agreed, and we made the eight hour trip up to Kibogora to assist him on this VIP patient. Dr. Al was that kind of a guy. He wanted everything to be just right in order to operate on his head nurse.

When the day came Dr. Al and I found everything in readiness with the scrub nurse getting the instruments ready, and the anesthetist all set with the anesthetic agents. The patient was lying supine on the operating table. Both Dr. Al and I were at her side about to go to the scrub sink just outside the operating room when the sheet over Dorothy was removed from the abdomen.

We had a good laugh. We saw a felt marker drawing of dash marks down the middle of Dorothy's abdomen where the operation was to be. Written next to it was "CUT HERE". She grinned up at us. This was a typical Dorothy Orcutt stunt. She had a good sense of humor which is surely needed when working in a developing country (or anywhere life takes you, for that matter).

Incidentally, the operation went well and our VIP patient made a good recovery. After a few days Maxine and I returned to work at Kibuye Hospital in Burundi.

Another unlikely medical problem which I would not encounter in the States is a stab wound due to machete or cow horn. One time a young boy fell out of a tree while holding a *panga* (machete). (He was likely cutting branches for firewood). He fell on the machete which penetrated his abdomen. Fortunately, he had no serious internal injuries and did well after the exploratory operation.

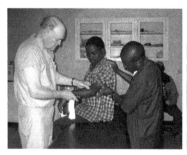 

FO examining a fractured arm   FO with boy who fell out of a tree with machete

Lack of Equipment –Mother of Invention

When I began working at Kibuye in 1970 there was some basic equipment such as a portable x-ray machine and a generator to power electric lights in the operating room. Gradually, over the years we were able to add equipment and machines, thanks to the Kare Kontainer Ministry in my home Conference (Pacific Northwest Conference of the Free Methodist Church).

A dedicated layman of the Lynnwood, Washington FMC coordinated donations from many sources and organized work parties to pack the containers. This friend, Duane Grooters, gave hours and hours to this ministry, arranging for the containers to be housed on the property of his employer at Glen's Welding in Lynnwood. For twenty years Duane and other volunteers faithfully collected, packed and shipped containers to Central Africa

Thousands of dollars were raised to send these huge shipments which generally took three to six months in transit. A sample route was: Lynnwood (Seattle) to Houston, then by ship to Dar es Salaam, Tanzania on Africa's east coast. After clearing customs–sometimes a lengthy process–the container would be loaded onto a truck and hauled inland some 700 miles to either Kibuye, Kibogora or Nundu.

Some of the equipment that came in containers had been donated by hospitals which were upgrading their own equipment. We gladly received hand-crank operating tables, not dependent on electricity, for example. Smaller items such as pulse-oximeters, BP cuffs and stethoscopes, lab equipment, and surgical instruments were all appreciated.

Duane and his wife Jerilyn made a visit to Nundu and Kibuye in 2008, seeing the fruits of this Kare Kontainer ministry. Jerilyn was thrilled to sit down and use the treadle sewing machine at Nundu – the very machine that she and Duane had purposely transported from Minnesota to Washington to send to Africa in one of the containers.

Of course there were still many modern things lacking, one of which was a fracture table which we use in the US for setting a broken hip. This type of fracture was not uncommon. I had to improvise, so I devised this method: First, I tied the operating table to a water pipe on one side of the room. Second, I folded a sheet corner-wise, put it between the legs and up over the shoulder of the patient to tie him or her on the table.

Then I used my nylon tow strap (taken from the shop). Usually this is used to hook onto a vehicle for towing. But I found it useful in the OR, by tying it to the ankle, then hooking the other end to my come-along (hand winch) which was attached to the door frame on the other side of the room. In this way I was able to lever it a few times in order to pull the leg out to the right length so I could do the operation. Of course, I did this under spinal anesthesia, so I did not hurt the patient.

Later, I was able to get a boat winch to replace the come-along. Jim Stillman, our maintenance man, drilled holes in the end of the OR table to install this, so I was able with a few turns of the winch to pull the leg out to the proper length. Also, I didn't need to tie the table to the water pipe anymore. This was a big improvement. At our visit in 2017 that apparatus is still in use at Kibuye Hope Hospital.

When the new hospital was built in 1978 we gained a second operating room. I needed a light over the table so I made one from materials at hand. It was the only time I welded things myself, since I usually had better welders available. I started with a heavy truck wheel and laid it flat on the floor. Next, I welded an old steel bed rail vertically on it.

Then I needed an arm that would pivot so I took the folding hardware of an old US Army stretcher and bolted it to the top of the bed rail. The final part was attaching a 12 volt spot light from a car to the end of that flexible arm. I wired it up to my battery system in the next room that was charged from the solar panels installed on the roof. This gave us light in our second operating room which was used for emergency C-sections when the main OR was in use. We often did minor surgery, dental extractions and endoscopy in that room. We also used it to prepare patients for surgery in Room One.

New Kibuye Hospital with Frank's father
surveying the progress, 1978

Mothers at well baby clinic, Kibuye Hospital

Nkondo church

Maxine Ogden hosting church leaders

With my batteries in the adjacent room, I also had an inverter to change the 12 volt direct current to 110 volt alternating current to run my cautery machine and other US-made equipment in the main OR. My lights there worked on either 12 volt DC or 110 volt AC.

For patients being treated in traction for different fractures we had coffee cans of different sizes filled with concrete. My team had welded special frames for mounting the weighted cans with a rope-pulley attached to the fractured limb.

Ladies (and sometimes men) in the US & Canada made rolls of bandages for us from old bed sheets, which sometimes came by the barrel full (old oil drums) in the shipping container. The groups that usually rolled these special bandages were part of the Women's Missionary International (WMI) organization of the Free Methodist Church. We called these special bandages "WMI gauze." They served to bandage thousands of wounds over the years. We often washed them to use again on jobs in the garden or around the house. Sometimes they showed up in bizarre places such as mending a fence, repairing a tear in a plastic bag, or at the market in town.

Friends and Family Come Alongside

Along with sending supplies to further the work of medical missions, some churches sent people. Two couples came to help us in Africa at different times, staying for long periods. Good friends Dan and Linda Corn (Bellingham, Washington) lived with us for a year when our time was divided between Nundu and Kibuye. Dan repaired and maintained equipment on each of those mission stations, working alongside the African maintenance men. Linda, RN, assisted me in the OR.

Later on, Lee and Vera Grantier (Madras, Oregon) volunteered for two years. They had their own apartment at Kibuye, a stone's throw from our home. Lee was my right hands for mechanical needs, and taught the mission station leaders how to maintain vehicles and other equipment. Vera kept the treadle sewing machine busy.

Malcolm and Bette Scott (Lancashire, England) also served at Kibuye for two years–Bette as a nurse and Malcolm as general handyman.

During our first term in Africa my brother Milt brought his entire family to visit us – wife Karolyn and four children. In those days we did all our communication through snail mail letters. We thought all the plans were in order but there was a snafu. We had driven our car the one thousand miles to Nairobi, Kenya to meet their plane, but they failed to arrive. We had no way of knowing what had happened so we started the long road trip back home to Burundi. We stopped for the night to camp at Serengeti National Park in Tanzania – still two hundred miles of rough dirt road ahead of us.

Our fellow missionary friend from Burundi, Ed Diely, just *happened* to be camped right next to us. He walked over to our camp site, saying, "We are really surprised to see you here! Didn't you know your brother and family are at Kibuye looking for you?"

"No! We thought we were to meet them in Nairobi, and they failed to show up. We've been taking our time touring animal parks in Tanzania on our way back home."

With this startling news we packed up early the next morning and drove on home to greet Milt and his family. For some reason they had flown into Bujumbura, not to Nairobi; a miscommunication of some kind. When we finally got together everything was fine. Our children enjoyed playing with their cousins, showing them the many wonders of African life. One of those small children, my niece Cynthia, later became an internist. She even returned to Kibuye as a fourth-year medical student to gain experience and to help me in the OR.

Chapter 7
THIRD MISSIONARY JOURNEY

In 1985 it was time to leave my practice of medicine & surgery in Centralia, Washington and return to missionary service in Africa. This time Maxine and I went alone as all three children were out of the nest. Our assignment at this point was to Kibogora Hospital. Dr. Al Snyder, missionary surgeon, was due to come on home assignment for a year, so I was asked by the mission to fill in for him at that time. I agreed to go, with the provision that I could have more French language study. I felt quite deficient in my language ability, having had only high school French plus a little tutoring during my first eight weeks in Africa. On top of that, I had been home for seven years, not speaking any French.

I requested to do this study at Laval University in Quebec City, Canada. I was counting on three or four months of concentrated study. The mission said yes to this plan but Dr. Snyder requested us to "take the six week course and arrive by August 22." I agreed to shorten my course, if the mission would allow us to take two more months of French study following our year at Kibogora. This was Okayed so Maxine and I headed for Quebec and took the 6 week course. We were accompanied by our daughter Ronda, and our niece Karen (daughter of my brother Phil). The two girls then returned to college at Roberts Wesleyan in North Chili, New York, while Maxine and I flew on to

Africa for the one year assignment at Kibogora. It was now August 1985.

We jumped into the work again, this time at Kibogora, taking Dr. Snyder's place for a year. Kibogora was a very active mission station at the time. Not only was there a growing hospital, but two secondary schools, a literature center and a large mother church with many outlying chapels. It was a busy place. Twenty-some missionaries lived "on the hill" that year, including seven children. There were doctors, nurses, mechanics, teachers and our resident linguist, Betty Ellen Cox, who translated Christian literature into the local language, Kinyarwanda, and gave grammar lessons to new missionaries. Short term workers came and went, while long term families had been there for years. Maxine, not having our children to care for, had a variety of roles— helping with mission accounts, hospital supply inventory and lending a hand in the Missionary Kid (MK) School.

Meanwhile, in neighboring Burundi, things were heating up politically, making it increasingly difficult for foreigners to work there, so Dr. David Crandall left the mission to rejoin the US Army. This left Kibuye Hospital without a doctor. Our Area Director for Africa, Jim Kirkpatrick (not to be confused with Charles Kirkpatrick, General Missionary Secretary at the time), asked if we would make visits to Kibuye during our time at Kibogora in order to help the nurses carry on the work there. We did this several times, making trips to our sister hospital in the neighboring country, ten to fourteen days each time. Being medical personnel and already well known in Burundi made these trips possible, although most foreigners were not being granted visas at this time.

Then our other sister hospital, Nundu in Zaire (DRC) asked for my help. Dr. Tim Kratzer, internist with infectious disease specialty, requested that I visit Nundu periodically, since he was not a surgeon. He would save surgical cases for me, so we went down to Nundu for a week or two on several occasions. These three Free Methodist hospitals, in three adjacent countries, are approx. an eight-hour drive apart, depending on delays at the international border, car trouble or other mishaps. We usually took two days to make the journey, stopping in Bujumbura for supplies. I called myself the gypsy surgeon of Central Africa that year.

On one of these visits Dr. Kratzer had gathered a lot of elective cases. After each operation I was drained physically, having perspired profusely from wearing surgical gown, mask, gloves, etc. I would lie down in the office and drink a Coke in order to proceed with the next patient and not be dehydrated. By the end of the day it was difficult to walk up the hill to the house which was not far away.

Further French Study

When Dr. Al returned to Kibogora, Maxine and I flew to Europe for vacation, followed by my promised two-month French course. We were enrolled in a language school in Lausanne, Switzerland; but our first stop was Brussels, Belgium where we bought a used Austin Princess. We drove this to England for a few days to visit friends.

In Preston we visited Jim & Ann Etherington, the parents of our friend and colleague Sheila, a nurse at Kibogora Hospital. We were having trouble with the cooling system on the car, so Jim took it to be fixed by a mechanic that he knew; and we took the train to Glasgow and Dumbarton, Scotland in order to go to Loch Lomond for a short cruise on that beautiful lake. We picked up our repaired car, then we ferried back to Belgium, picking up Ronda and niece Karen in Amsterdam. In this way, we had a nice family vacation, driving through picturesque Germany on our way to Switzerland.

Once in Lausanne, we settled into the home of a Swiss family, arranged by the language school. The idea was French immersion so we could learn it well. It was interesting (and God's provision) that our hostess had two sons who were medical students, living at home, so we were with them at mealtimes. When they heard how my left arm was tingling whenever I turned my head to the left, one of them suggested I see a neurosurgeon at the medical school. In fact, he came home the next day and said,

"I made an appointment for you to see the doctor. Of course, you can cancel if you don't want to go."

Maxine said, "No way are you canceling; you are going!"

After the doctor examined me he ordered tests—electromyography and cervical myelography. The myelogram was done at the radiologist's office, and I went right home afterward. This resulted in a bad spinal headache. If you stay lying down, the pain is not severe; but *sitting or standing* is really bad. The day after the myelogram I was to give a talk in French class on some medical topic. Here's what I did to avoid the terrible headache: The trailer of the bus going to school had a bench seat on which I could lie down; and in class they put three chairs together, so I could lie down in order to give my speech. The following day I did not go to class. The tests showed a ruptured disk in my neck. The surgeon there was ready to operate, but I didn't want to be in Switzerland, recovering in someone else's home. I wanted to go to Seattle and home to have the operation done by.my friend and medical school classmate, Dr. Ralph Kamm, neurosurgeon.

I recovered enough from the spinal headache to drive to Augsburg, Germany where Dr. David Crandall was now stationed in the US Army. He agreed to sell our car for us, and he put us on the plane to Seattle. Dr. Kamm confirmed the problem as outlined in Switzerland. He took some bone from my hip; removed the damaged disk and put the bone graft in to cause the fusion in my neck. The symptoms went away almost immediately. Maxine and I stayed in our home at Lake Cavanaugh for my recovery, then returned to Africa after Christmas 1986.

Return to Africa

Now that Dr. Snyder was back at Kibogora we did not need two surgeons there, and Nundu was crying for help. We loaded our things on the mission Daihatsu truck and drove it the 200+ miles on terrible roads to Nundu. We initially stayed in a little two-room apartment. Later we had a three-bedroom house. We had no air conditioning, but we did have a ceiling fan over our bed in order to sleep at night. It was battery-powered, so it worked after the generator was turned off at night.

We began using the new operating room before the air conditioner was installed. Once again, I took my little 12-Volt truck fan to the OR to help move the air. OR personnel get so hot having to wear gowns, masks and gloves for sterile purposes Once the AC unit was installed we noticed a remarkable improvement. This made the surgery much easier.

One of the more interesting situations in our service at Nundu was the time I was so ill that I had to "break scrub" and lie on a gurney (stretcher) while Dr. Kratzer finished the operation with my direction. That problem has only happened twice in my 50-year career. (The other time was simpler at Kibuye. I just lay on a gurney in the operating room and coached the whole operation done by the national physician). Another time when I was ill, I still managed to do ten gastroscopies, an emergency C-section and I cared for a ruptured uterus. I was barely able to drag myself up the Kibogora hill to return to bed at 11:00p.m.

One day a fisherman near Nundu accidently put gasoline in his kerosene lamp to go out fishing at night. It exploded and he was severely burned, over nearly half of his body. Our only general anesthetic available was Ketamine. In rare occasions this causes a very agitated response so the patient was struggling to get off the operating table. We had to tie him down and it was a very difficult debridement and dressing with Silvadene ointment. This was in the old operating room without AC. The entire procedure was long, hot and with an agitated patient.

During the time at Nundu we made several visits to Kibuye to help that medical program which was lacking a doctor. Finally, it was secure enough to live at Kibuye again so we moved back to Burundi. Besides this, the road to Nundu was so terrible that my back was suffering each time we made the journey. I still made several trips to Nundu because of their need for a surgeon.

Much of the time I was the only doctor at Kibuye, but sometimes the government sent us a national physician which really helped my work load. However, more than once, after working with me for some months, the Ministry of Health would send these doctors to serve in a government hospital elsewhere. One who was able to stay for some time, Dr. Canisius Havyarimana, built on what I had taught him by going to France for formal training in surgery. He is now serving as a surgeon in Bujumbura.

Dr, Audifax is another who worked with me for a year before being assigned elsewhere by the Ministry of Health. However, we really needed someone to stick with us at Kibuye. In 2005 I retired from full-time service, turning over the care of Kibuye Hospital to Dr. Eraste Mukenga. He was assisted by part-time physicians Dr. Diane Kaneza and Elisee Nahimana who had other jobs elsewhere. After a few years Mukenga left Kibuye to be the personal physician for the President of Burundi, Pierre Nkurunziza.

We were privileged to entertain American ambassadors from time to time, making friends with them. When in Bujumbura we were able to swim in the pool at the ambassador's residence. We also met some of the presidents of Burundi: President Bugaza came to see the new hospital being built at Kibuye in 1978. We sat down together in the unfinished operating room and talked about the medical program in our area of the country. Some three decades later President Nkurunziza toured the hospital and helped plant fruit trees around the complex.

Frank & Maxine with US Ambassador Cynthia Perry c1990

Busoma

In 1990 I saw that infants in Burundi were having trouble making the transition from mother's milk to regular diet. This is a critical time for children to get enough protein and grow well. Many were dying due to malnutrition. I learned of a cereal made from sorghum, soy beans and corn. I modified the recipe slightly and produced it at Kibuye and Muyebe. I named it BUSOMA, an anachronism: BU stands for the country of Burundi, SO for Sorghum & Soybeans, and MA for Maize (French for corn). It also contains a small amount of sugar. It's a very nutritional hot cereal, with the soybeans providing the necessary protein.

Busoma is used widely throughout the country of Burundi. Initially, the plant was powered by a diesel generator; but now we have hydro-electric power or solar power, so the generator is only used during power outages. After the three grains are cleaned and toasted the sugar is added, then all is milled together into a fine flour. It is then packaged in half kilo bags with instructions for boiling in water for eight minutes. This cereal is used in the feeding programs at Kibuye Hope Hospital (KHH) and Muyebe Clinic where parents are taught nutrition and proper use of Busoma. We are grateful for the dedicated staff who make and distribute this life-saving product.

Sorghum being prepared for Busoma cereal

Milling Busoma grains at Kibuye

Nicknames

Our African hospital staff would often give us special names in the local language. Dr. Snyder, as both medical director at Kibogora, and chairman of the mission in Rwanda, was called *Bideri* the name of a chief.

"Do you know what the African staff call you?" asked Dr. Al Snyder, as we scrubbed together for an operation.

"No, I don't, I replied.

"Kibugita, which as you know, means Big Knife. But they wouldn't want you to know."

Some days later I was in the Operating Room setting up for surgery. I turned to Suzanne, my head nurse, and said "I know the nickname you call me–*Kibugita."*

"Oh!" she said. "You weren't supposed to know that!" She was very embarrassed.

"I don't mind at all," I replied. "It's just fine." *In fact, I took it as a compliment*.

My staff recognized that I often do seven operations in a day, sometimes followed by emergency surgery in the night. This, besides seeing patients between operations and making ward rounds. Fortunately, not all days were like that, or I would have worn out. Not to mention keeping enough instruments sterilized for that many procedures.

Another reason Big Knife works for me is the way I deal with patients who come in with shock. I have, on occasion, rushed a patient to the operating room; opened him up; and stopped the bleeding to get him out of shock (sometimes the only way to save him). This is particularly appropriate when you don't have a blood bank. Some surgeons I have known in the US will not operate until the patient can be gotten out of shock. I saw that when I was a junior resident.

I was able to save a young man who had collided with a mailbox on his motorcycle. When we opened him we discovered a rupture of the right ventricle of his heart, and I covered the hole with my left index finger. At the same time I placed the first suture under my finger to close the one-centimeter defect and stop the small geyser that occurred with each heartbeat. We had him in the OR in under ten minutes from arrival in the emergency room. We were able to transfuse him and he did well. That happened in Modesto, California.

In that same hospital, during my last year in surgical residency, my instructor was Dr. Paul Carlson. He taught me to be a fast surgeon, to anticipate several moves ahead in the procedures and not delay in getting the work done. This became very good for me in Africa. I was often able to do seven major operations in a day. I usually scheduled three or four major procedures, but emergency cases would arrive and be added to the roster.

Sometimes the elective procedures were put off until the next day, even if it were Saturday. Most often the emergency would be a C-section, as those are not usually scheduled. Those went pretty fast. Often the baby was in distress, so quick surgery was essential. I would have the nurse anesthetist give IV Ketamine and have the baby out in three minutes and be totally finished in twenty minutes. Once I did it in twelve minutes. These experiences in the OR helped explain my

African nickname, *Kibugita,* Big Knife, and also led to my second nickname, *Flying Object*.

Sometimes central supply was just not able to get enough surgical packs and instruments sterilized for so many operations. I have been known to work using drapes that were sterilized but still quite wet, and once I had to scrub very quickly and had sterile gloves but no gown. I always had a plastic apron; but it was not sterile, so I just avoided getting against the table.

At Kibuye two nurses would scrub with me for every operation. On peptic ulcers or C-sections they knew exactly what instrument I needed next, so I would just extend my right hand and the instrument would be right there; and for suturing, the needle holder would be loaded correctly with the right suture. Both Matthew Hacimana and Jean Dukundane (Duk for short) were especially good at that.

Part of the time during the years in Burundi, Rwanda and Zaire (Congo) we were able to talk between mission stations by short-wave radio. We did not use our regular names, rather, the code used in aviation. Thus, my initials F O made me Foxtrot Oscar, but because I was a rapid surgeon; had my hands into repairing many things and developing solar installations in houses and hospitals, etc. Dr. Snyder changed my code name to *Flying Object*. This became my nickname among the mission family.

Chapter 8

HOME ASSIGNMENT
AND BAD NEWS

I n May 1993 Maxine flew home ahead of me in order to be with Ronda, and I followed in June. This was our regular home rotation in which we would normally travel together visiting our supporting churches and representing Free Methodist World Missions. This Home Assignment was quite different.

How I Almost Died

In early September I developed severe abdominal pain in the night and collapsed when I tried to get out of bed. The ambulance was called and I was carried down the 43 steps of our home (at Lake Cavanaugh) to our car and driven by Maxine to the hospital in Sedro Woolley. In the morning my surgeon friend, Dr. Morris Johnson, was called; and I was transferred to Skagit Valley Hospital in Mount Vernon. Tests were done, and it was determined that my gall bladder was infected instead of my appendix. It was so bad that laparoscopic cholecystectomy failed, so they opened up and removed a *very* bad gall bladder as well as my appendix. I then went into septic shock. They bailed me out of that with many liters of IV fluids into pulmonary edema; then with diuretics got the fluid out of my lungs, and I didn't die after all. God was with me. Had that happened at Kibuye I most certainly would have died. Even in the United States septic shock had a 50 percent mortality at that time.

Maxine's Cancer

My recovery delayed a scheduled operation for Maxine which we thought was a Spigelian hernia. When they operated on her they found instead a cancer of the right colon. It was resected, but it had already invaded the abdominal wall. This started her three year battle against cancer. While taking care of her, I also worked part of the time as a surgical assistant for a group of surgeons in Mount Vernon, including Dr. Johnson.

Genocide in two countries

Besides coping with these illnesses we were reading in the newspaper about another genocide in Burundi following the assassination of the Hutu President Ndadiye by some Tutsi soldiers on October 21, 1993. Many nurses, church workers and other educated Hutus were hunted down and massacred by the military in reprisal for Tutsis killed after Ndadiye was slain. It was difficult to learn of these things from afar. (No internet or e-mail.) Missionary personnel who were at Kibuye at the time were flown out by army helicopter. These included Dr. Norman and Laurene Zook; Jim and Barbara Stillman; and Debbie Hogeboom. Later, we would hear stories from our Burundian employees of how they escaped death by hiding or fleeing. One eye witness told of the senseless slaughter of thirteen beloved Burundian friends, including the District Superintendent & some of his children. They were buried in a mass grave near our home at Kibuye.

The Red Cross came and used our Kibuye Hospital to care for victims who were still alive. After the Red Cross left I was called to help re-establish the work of the hospital in January 1994. I stayed only one month because Maxine was entering radiotherapy for her cancer; in fact, they started a week earlier than we had expected, and she was really ill by the time I returned home.

Maxine's final trip to Africa

In 1995 Maxine was in remission with the cancer, so we packed our bags to return to Kibogora Hospital for three months. The genocide of Rwanda had begun in April 1994. This war, like the one in Burundi, was also between the Hutu and Tutsi tribes. The media made it sound like Tutsis were the only victims, but the truth is, there were thousands of deaths on both sides; we lost both Hutu and Tutsi friends in both Burundi and Rwanda.

I was one of the first doctors to return to re-establish the medical care at Kibogora Hospital. Drs. John Brose and Paul Embree had preceded me for short periods. We could still hear gunfire at night. I had a police escort when I was called for emergencies in the night. I had much to do in the hospital with many injured plus the normal things that happen in a general hospital. Once again, I was the only surgeon.

Maxine, along with Gladys Schlosser, worked on getting the houses back in good condition, as they had been ransacked by looters during the war. They sewed sheets to cover windows, made sofa cushions & pillows. They also made surgical gowns and drapes—replacing many important items that had been stolen with the breakdown of law and order. They also cleared up the contents of filing cabinets and bookshelves which we found dumped on the floor in the mission houses and schoolhouse. It was quite a mess.

Our final months with Maxine

When we returned from that period of service we decided to take a trip around the USA in our Plymouth Acclaim. It was September, a beautiful time of year to tour the country. Maxine had wanted to do this and she was well enough, though getting weaker. We travelled 9,000 miles through 26 states visiting many friends and relatives and seeing interesting sites. We visited Teddy Roosevelt National Park in North Dakota. That was the 50th state that I have visited.

I was glad that we made this trip, as soon Maxine's cancer returned in force. She was able to partici-pate in the wedding of our daughter, Ronda, to Dana Davies, on January 27, 1996. I sang the "The Lord's Prayer" after giving her away. I had sung the same song at son Wesley's wedding to Mary Hale in Deer Flat, Idaho in 1980.

As a wedding gift to Dana & Ronda we took a Holland America cruise with them on the Mexican Riviera. Maxine spent most of her time in a wheel chair and did not go ashore with the rest of us, but cruising was good thing to do when she had limited mobility. She could still enjoy all the wonderful activities on board. It was so good to see our youngest happily married, and to get better acquainted with our son-in-law on this trip.

On December 3, 1996 God saw fit to take my beloved wife of 39 years to glory. I had known for nine months that aside from divine intervention Maxine would not survive this cancer. When her final day came, Ronda and I were at her side at our home at Lake Cavanaugh. (It had been our cabin since 1975 and our home base since 1985 when I left practice in Centralia. We had improved it over the years so it was a real home.) We had a memorial service at our Mt. Vernon FM Church; then I took the train to Salem, Oregon to visit Gene & Jocelyn VanBrocklin. As close friends for many years they could help me know what next to do with my life now that I was alone.

Chapter 9

A NEW SONG

In January 1997, I took a one-month assignment with the mission, serving again at Kibogora Hospital, this time alone. As I pondered my future, I felt I could not work for the mission in Africa for long periods by myself, and that God would provide a new help-mate for me. I knew Carol Watson, a single missionary who was a dedicated servant of Christ. She had served for ten years in our mission in Rwanda and at this time was working at the FM World Missions office in Indianapolis due to the genocide which caused her to be evacuated with other expatriates in April 1994. Carol already knew French and Kinyarwanda, similar to Kirundi, and we were supported by many of the same churches in the Pacific Northwest.

It was during this short-term at Kibogora that I was praying in the middle of the night, asking God for a new wife while thinking about Carol. I was reading Psalm 40 in the Living Bible and verse three jumped out to me in a *very* special way. *"He has given me a new song to sing, of praises to our God."* I knew then that God would answer my prayer, and that Carol would be the new wife to help me continue serving Him in Africa. Later I realized that "carol" means song. She would be my *"new* song". I visited her in Indianapolis for three days on my way home from Africa and sent her a fre-quent-flyer ticket to Seattle.

Over the next two months we got to know each other through phone calls and snail mail letters, then we spent some days together, when she flew home to Seattle for Easter vacation. One of our outings took us to Cannon Beach, Oregon. It happened to be Good Friday.

Carol tells the story: *"We were walking on the beach—and I decided to write a love note in the sand. I wrote: I LOVE F.O. Frank took the stick and wrote: MARRY ME. Though I had been praying for two months to know God's will in this matter, my answer came right then and there. I sensed the Lord saying 'Go ahead and take a leap of faith and trust Me'. So I confidently took the stick again and wrote: OK! Frank grabbed me in a fierce hug and said 'Oh honey, I'm so happy!' A great peace flooded over me after eight weeks of emotional ups and downs."*

We returned to Salem to share the good news with our hosts Gene & Jocelyn VanBrocklin. That was Friday. Saturday we had an engagement dinner with family & friends. Sunday, which was Easter, we drove back to Seattle to tell our folks that we were engaged. We also planned our wedding that afternoon before Carol had to fly back to Indiana on Monday. It was quite a weekend!

On Sunday June 8th we were married during the morning worship service at Carol's home church, First FMC, campus church of SPU. As a surprise to us, the service began with choir director Ron Haight leading the singers down the center aisle swaying and singing "Siyahamba" in Zulu. They then switched to English as the congregation was invited to join in singing, "We are walking in the light of God". It was truly a moving start for the wedding service of us two Africa missionaries on the front row. Pastor Mark Abbott led a wonderful service; his message was about partnership with God and brought out how both Frank and Carol had partnered with God for many years and now would be partnering together in continued service to God in Africa.

Missionary Service with Carol

Our first place to serve the mission together was the Pacific Coast Japanese Conference (PCJC) family camp near Redwood City, CA. This appointment for Carol had been made some months earlier, so she had called the superintendent and asked, "Can you take two missionaries for the price of one? I am about to marry Dr. Frank Ogden, fellow missionary from Rwanda and Burundi." Of course he agreed, so we flew to San Francisco and presented our work and future plans. Carol could still speak some Japanese from being a missionary in Japan years before; but of course, these Nisei Japanese knew English. They enjoyed learning "Jesus Loves Me" in Kirundi, *Yesu Arankunda.*

It was a busy summer besides the PCJC camp. Some months earlier, before my engagement to Carol, I had committed to a medical-dental mission team to China. Now that my plans had changed the team leader tried, but couldn't find another doctor to replace me. I left my bride of six weeks and flew to Beijing with the team to minister in rural China (Manchuria Province). I was able to fly home a day early and surprise her, as she returned from representing the mission at a youth retreat in Colorado. We rented a small U Haul truck to move Carol from Indianapolis to our home at Lake

Cavanaugh, Washington. We had six weeks of further speaking engagements before returning to Africa as a married couple in October, 1997.

Our first overseas assignment together was to Kibogora Hospital because the civil war in Burundi was still simmering and security was an issue. Our African friends were happy to see that God had given me a new wife, and someone they already knew! (Carol had spent six months at Kibogora as a new missionary learning Kinyarwanda in 1985-86). And they were thrilled to see how God had finally given Carol a husband. This was a time of healing for her, as she found plenty of Rwandan friends who had survived the genocide. We were both so thankful for God's provision and direction.

I was quite busy in the work of the hospital. This time I had two national physicians, Georges Ntakiyiruta and Beata Mukarugwiro (husband and wife). I was able to teach Georges a lot of surgery, and he was a good student who later went on for full training in surgery. Carol began teaching English in the two nearby high schools, assisting the hospital chaplain on his rounds, and speaking in churches in the area when invited.

Although immersed in the medical scene at Kibogora, the situation of Kibuye Hospital was still on my heart, so we made visits to Burundi several times, even though rebels were still controlling some areas. We drove Carol's old Nissan Patrol on our first visit and were able to get my 1986 Volvo sedan out of storage at Mweya Mission. Ed Kirkpatrick helped us get it running after being up on blocks for five years.

On one of these journeys into Burundi we got a flat tire on the Volvo and our jack wouldn't work. We were the only vehicle on the road in the late afternoon and we knew this territory was held by rebels at night. But God was with us in a marvelous way. After a few minutes of wondering what to do, a well-dressed African man drove up asking if we needed help. He not only had the right jack but assisted in changing the tire. Then he drove off, refusing any money for his kind service. His was the only vehicle on the road besides ours. We still think of him as an angel sent by God.

Due to the insecurity, on these one-to-two week visits to Burundi, we would spend our nights in a guest house in Gitega, twenty miles away from the hospital. Later in 2001 and 2003 while staying at our home at Kibuye, we were robbed at gunpoint four times. We gave these rebel soldiers some money and our camera, so we were not injured any time. (Most of our funds were safe because we hid them in clever places, like the inside of a jigsaw puzzle box in a cupboard of games.) Frightening as these invasions were, God was with us, giving us the right words to say to these young men. Their war was not with us; they were merely hungry and trying to find provisions.

Carol and I continued to serve the mission together full time for eight years, retiring from "career" status in June of 2005. I was nearing 70 years of age. In anticipation of our leaving I was training national physicians to take over; namely, Dr. Eraste Mukenga. In a "handing over" ceremony I placed a stethoscope around Dr. Mukenga's neck, and he presented me with a wooden plaque he had commissioned. It depicts us two doctors facing each other, with me putting a larger-than-life stethoscope around his neck, just like I had done moments before. (See Dr. Mukenga's story in Appendix 1.)

Following that official break, and having turned Kibuye Hospital over to Dr. Mukenga as the new medical director, we returned to the USA, promising to come back to Africa on a short term basis. After a year and a half we did just that. We returned to Kibuye to work for two to three months a year, taking work teams with us each time to provide expertise in various areas, and to encourage the ongoing work in the aftermath of war. During this semi-retirement season we were busy recruiting other physicians to go in my place, as there were still very few African doctors in Burundi at this time. We also traveled to churches and camps speaking about God's work in Central Africa.

In the summer of 2006 Carol and I were the missionary speakers at Warm Beach Family Camp, not far from our home at Lake Cavanaugh. As usual, the featured missionaries were asked to choose a project to be funded by the camp offerings. Throughout my career in Africa I had been trying to gradually upgrade the services where I have worked. This was the perfect opportunity to get some new equipment. I chose a small, portable ultrasound machine that I could take as part of our baggage when we returned to Africa the next time.

I made the purchase before camp so I could show it to the congregation. I also thought I should try out this new machine at home before taking it overseas, so I had Carol lie down while I examined her abdomen with the new ultrasound.

"Oh, I see you have an ovarian cyst!" That was news to Carol and me both. She had no idea anything was amiss. Some women get these cysts which cause no problem. Many resolve on their own. We went to see a gynecologist in Mount Vernon. As the doctor looked at Carol on her machine she agreed there was an ovarian cyst.

"Although this isn't an emergency, I advise you to have this taken out because you're heading for Africa soon." This type of cyst can get twisted, causing awful pain and requiring an emergency operation. "We can have the ovaries removed laparoscopically and have you home the same or following day, she added."

The scheduled date for the operation turned out to be the Friday of camp week. Two days later we were invited to the platform during the Sunday morning service just before the missionary offering was taken. I carried the ultrasound machine to the podium and showed it to the audience of some 500 people. Carol was standing with me, as I told the above story.

"You see that Carol is here just two days after her operation. She looks pretty good, doesn't she? This machine is going to be a big help at Kibuye Hospital. Thank you to all for making this possible. It will be used for years to come, especially in difficult maternity cases which we see frequently."

Friends Lend a Hand

We took small teams with us to helpe at both Kibuye and Kibogora. These included medical personnel, engineers, mechanics, computer specialists, photographers and prayer partners. Two families deserve special mention because they helped with the restoration of many damaged or stolen items due to war.

Gene & Jocelyn VanBrocklin (Salem, Oregon) spent six months with us (Nov. 1998 to April 1999) at both Kibogora and Kibuye. Gene repaired many broken doors and windows at Kibuye. He also installed a new 12-volt light in the operating room. Jocelyn sewed Naugahyde mattress covers with Carol. Most all the mattresses on our hospital beds had been stolen. We could buy foam mattresses, but needed waterproof covers that could be cleaned.

In the summer of 1998 Jeff & Anne Yerger (Olympia, Washington) with daughters Julie, 18 and Kristy, 16 were a huge help to us for two months, both at Kibuye and at Kibogora. Many things got repaired, replaced, resewn, sorted and cleaned following the looting at the hospital and missionary homes. Interesting side note: Nine years later Julie became a career missionary nurse at Kibogora Hospital. Jeff and Anne made numerous trips in a ten-year period to Kibogora to help in practical ways.

I am very grateful for a team of American dentists that came several different times—Drs. Burton (Helen) Hodges and Ed (Shirley) Davenport from Michigan. They brought their portable equipment with them and used our air compressor from the shop. Their wives assisted them.

Others came for two months at a time, like Frank and Sylvia Hallenbeck, and Keith and Lois Snyder, both from New York State. The Snyders' stay coincided with two historic events: The arrival of mainline electricity at Kibuye; and the attack on the twin towers in NYC

(9/11/2001). In fact, we learned about it while listening to BBC World News around the breakfast table on 9/12. It sounded at first like the reading of an Orson Wells fictitious story. Our African friends expressed condolence and were concerned that we might live near New York City.

Carol's 28-year old nephew, Nathan Watson, was visiting at the same time as the Snyders. Not only did he hear about 9-11 on BBC with us, but lived through some "exciting" times such as an attempted break-in one night by rebel soldiers (we were able to hand them some money through the screen door which satisfied them), and a scary drive through rebel-held territory when we were detoured due to reported active gun fire on our main route to Bujumbura.

More helper friends will be mentioned in Chapter ten.

Working with the Church in Rwanda and Burundi

From the beginning of my missionary career, I had a good working relationship with the local church. Each of the three hospitals I served–Kibogora, Kibuye, and Nundu–were under the auspices of the Free Methodist Church (FMC) in their respective countries. I was acquainted with a number of the superintendents, pastors and lay leaders, and it was a privilege to work closely with Bishops Noah Nzeyimana and Elie Buconyori in Burundi, Bishop Bya'ene Ilangi in Zaire, and Bishop Aaron Ruhumuriza in Rwanda.

Whether with Maxine or with Carol, I traveled to various churches, often taking a vehicle-load of church leaders who appreciated a ride to a far-flung congregation. Often 800-1000 people would gather for worship at the "mother" church for a special occasion such as a guest speaker.

When the AIDS epidemic was beginning in African countries, I was greatly concerned and prepared a talk, based on Scripture, which I presented in various churches. Even before we realized the disease could be transmitted by blood one of the lab workers at Kibuye died from handling contaminated blood. This brought home to us the seriousness of the disease. My "sermon" title was *"A Medical Crisis-A Human Disaster-An Evangelistic Opportunity."* AIDS is a disease of near one hundred percent fatality caused by promiscuous sexual activity. We didn't have any HIV medicines in those early days.

In African society AIDS comes with a definite sigma and rejection. However, it is an evangelistic opportunity as these people are very receptive to the Gospel knowing they will die. It is our responsibility as Christians to not reject them but point them to Jesus Christ. This is very much what we do in all of our hospitals in Central Africa. We hire chaplains who are more able to lead patients to Jesus Christ than we missionaries.

After I married Carol I was happy to turn over the speaking in local churches to her. She is an ordained minister and ready to preach or teach whenever invited. One Sunday at Kibuye we were preparing to go out the door to a rural church some distance away in Pastor Hacimana's District. Like others, he was a bi-vocational pastor, working at the hospital during the week while serving his church on the weekends. We usually filled our vehicle with local Christians on these church visits, including an interpreter for Carol since she is more comfortable preaching in English. Pastor Hacimana was very good in English and had agreed to help. Besides, it was *his* church we were visiting on this day.

Just as we were getting in the van a runner came from the hospital with a note saying Dr. Frank was needed for an emergency C-Section. Of course, Hacimana, as my right-hand assistant, was needed too, so we both changed into our scrubs, delivered the baby, changed back into church clothes, and were on our way with only a thirty minute delay. When we arrived, the congregation was singing and waiting to start the service. All in a day's work!

Every time we went to visit a distant church the local women would cook a meal for the church leaders and us following the service. Considering that the journey sometimes took an hour or more on difficult roads and the service was often two to three hours long, we really appreciated the meal before the long journey home. Many times we were presented with a live chicken, or a basket of eggs, some pineapples or a stalk of bananas. In rainy season we had some "adventures" getting stuck in the mud but our passengers would help push us out. Sometimes we used chains or threw branches under the wheels for traction.

Four Burundian lay leaders deserve special mention because of their faithful service and strategic roles during my years in Burundi. Japhet Nsanzerugeze was first sent to Kibuye by the Burundi FMC to be staff manager and bookkeeper of the hospital in 1985. Later he was sent to Nairobi, Kenya for accounting training which then led to his business degree. Japhet continued to serve the Church, even while in exile in Kenya for seven years (while Burundi was in civil war) and finally repatriated in 2001. Among other positions he held, Japhet served as Administrator of KHH for seventeen years.

Meanwhile, Pascal Bigirimana, nurse and pharmacist "held the fort" during five of the twelve years of civil unrest (1993-98) when there was no doctor in residence at Kibuye. Though the hospital was reduced to a dispensary level, Pascal treated patients with the limited medicines and supplies available. Other staff helped, and by God's grace the hospital stayed open during those difficult years. Pascal continued working at the hospital all through the troubled times, and beyond.

Helene Niyonizigye also provided continuity during Kibuye's history. Her faithful management of finances, supplies and personnel were vital in keeping medical services available to the community in uncertain times. She has been a stalwart at Kibuye, and continues her service to the hospital today, along with her husband Fidele.

Fidele Niyongabo has held various positions as a dedicated layman, most notably, his long tenure as manager of the Busoma Food Factory (see Chapter 7). With the assistance of Edouard Vyizigiro he managed to keep producing this nutritious food during the civil war years. Fidele also helped us missionaries with business matters, and served as interpreter on numerous occasions due to his excellent English.

Japhet Nsanzerugeze, long time KHH
administrator with wife Goretti

A New Song

Fidele Niyongabo, long time Busoma Manager with wife
Helene, long time worker in KHH business office

Pascal Bigirimana, long time pharmacist at KHH

Carol and I have compiled stories of other African Christians which we wrote some years ago, called "Heroes of the Faith". See Appendix 1.

Chaplain stories

Pastor Pascal Nyawenda has been a faithful chaplain at Kibuye Hospital for many years. He preaches boldly and simply and many respond. Here are a few of the encouraging reports we have heard through the years from Pascal. Others— pastors, chaplains, missionaries— have prayed with patients in all our hospitals, resulting in sins forgiven and lives transformed. Only Heaven can tell the full impact of medical care given in Jesus' Name.

One day a young man was diagnosed with AIDS. Chaplain Pascal helped him face his death well by accepting the forgiveness of Jesus Christ. He decided to straighten his life out for however long God would give him. He asked for a Bible and said he wanted to grow as a Christian. We now have some medicines to help HIV+ patients and he received that too. Spiritual awakening among patients happens frequently and makes our time here worthwhile, since the body is temporary but the soul lives forever. Pascal told us that nearly one hundred percent of the AIDS patients he counsels profess faith in Christ before going home to die.

Another time I diagnosed terminal cancer in a lady and referred her to the chaplain. He presented the gospel and God had prepared her heart to receive him for the first time. She met with him daily for follow up Bible lessons.

Another woman had demons that Chaplain Pascal cast out. He told me "She is really a pagan and Satan had a strong hold on her. I may need to chase those demons out again."

One man came to the hospital with TB. This is often an indication that the persons has AIDS. When he heard the Good news presented by Chaplain Pascal he accepted Christ right then and there. He had to stay for three more weeks of TB treatment, during which time he went to the chapel service every day when Chaplain Pascal preached to the outpatients in a large covered porch area. This patient was so eager to learn about his new faith that he asked for private Bible lessons. He gave his testimony in front of other patients. At the end of three weeks he was healed of the TB and went home rejoicing. He was now ready to meet his maker. This is really why we have medical work in Africa. Testimonies like this make it all worthwhile.

Getting Away From Work

Though I was the only doctor at our hospitals much of my career, that was not always the case; and even at those times I was able to get away for Sunday services at rural churches (as described above) or outings to a lake or waterfalls. Sometimes a trip got changed or even cancellation —to the chagrin of the family— due to an emergency at the hospital.

At different times I owned small motorcycles, and when fuel was available would take rides in the community with one or two of my kids along, or later with Carol. I don't think I ever convinced Maxine to accompany me on that machine. I was very careful—especially after a rainstorm. I did have a small accident on a log bridge with Carol along on my Honda 125. I was only going about five miles per hour, but the front wheel slipped into the groove between logs and we tipped over, landing in the ditch. She was not hurt, and my knee healed without problems. No crutches were needed.

At Kibuye I often rode my 1969 Honda 50 MiniTrail to the hospital, some six blocks away. I would not have to walk home after a long tiring day of operations, consultations, and ward rounds. It was rather comical the few times that Carol rode with me up the hill to the hospital. The locals laughed to see two adults on such a small "*moto*".

Bill and Wes learned to ride before they were old enough to drive a car. They often took one of their Burundian pals with them when riding the Kawasaki 90. They even taught Noah Nzeyimama to ride when he was a teenager. He later became the first bishop of the Burundi Free Methodist Church. Our boys enjoyed playing outdoor games with Burundian friends their ages, usually inventing what to do. One of them was Rusagi, who later became a faithful worker in the Busoma baby food plant. He's pictured pouring grain into the hammer mill in chapter 7.

We often had Friday game night at our house when we lived at Kibogora. Maxine and I would invite other missionaries for popcorn and a card game called Rook or other games. When Carol was single, living at Kibogora for six months of Kinyarwanda language study, she remembers well the knock at her door.

"Games & popcorn at our house tonight," she heard me announce, going from house to house.

Seven kilometers (four miles) from Kibogora was Kumbya Retreat Center on beautiful Lake Kivu. This was a safe place to swim. There were no hippos, crocodiles or Bilharzia caused by the parasite Schistosoma found in other places. Snakes were rarely seen, so we just watched for them and never saw one. The water was refreshingly cool, as the lake is at 5,000 feet elevation. Many Saturdays a mission vehicle would load up people and picnic supplies and spend the day at the beach.

Sunday night devotional gatherings in a missionary's home were helpful to recharge spiritually for the week ahead. It was good to sing and worship in English.

Change of Plans Due to War

Anyone living in a foreign culture will tell you that being flexible is one of the first things you learn. One time after being robbed we took an interesting vacation to Zanzibar, just off the coast of Tanzania. Here's what happened.

A group of rebels had invaded our home at night looking for food and money. Our leaders had told us that if this ever happened, we should cooperate so we would not be harmed. We did cooperate and let them in, rather than risking the door being broken down or worse. Although they did not hurt us physically, we still felt the trauma that comes from having armed strangers enter your home and hold you at gunpoint while opening drawers and cupboards looking for cash or food.

After they left we decided to get away for a week or two to recover. A spontaneous trip to Zanzibar filled the bill. These "Spice Islands" on the Indian Ocean are steeped in Arabic history, culture and architecture. We took a walking tour through a private grove of spice trees to see how cloves, nutmeg, cinnamon, and black pepper are grown and harvested. This short get-away renewed our spirits, so we could return to the work at Kibuye.

In 2002 when it seemed too insecure to return to Burundi we wondered what to do, but God had a plan and directed us to Malawi, another small country some 1,000 miles to the south. Carol was asked to teach in our Free Methodist Bible School in Lilongwe (now Great Commission Bible School) during the November 2002 and January 2003 modules. I worked in a clinic of another mission organization, African Bible College (ABC). What an encouragement to see another part of the worldwide church, alive and growing. We were also blessed to work alongside missionaries Len and Karen Roller who directed the school at that time.

While in Malawi we became friends with a German family, the Hoyncks. The father was a gynecologist at the government hospital in Lilongwe. One day Volker came to me and asked if I would evaluate his 16-year old son, Daniel, for possible appendicitis. I made the examination and concurred.

Then Volker said "Will you do the operation? I know a private mission hospital not far from town which would be better than where I work." We made the journey to this hospital that night and I removed a "hot" appendix, with Volker assisting. Because it was late we spent the night in the home of the South African missionary doctor, whose wife treated us with a hot meal at 9 PM following the surgery. The next morning we enjoyed Rooibos tea and rusks, South African specialties. Daniel did very well. (Incidentally, we visited the Hoyncks in eastern Germany nine years later. Daniel was by then married with one child. He and his wife were talking of immigrating to Israel to be missionaries.)

Following our time in Malawi we returned to Burundi, planning to settle in again at Kibuye for a long stretch, hoping for no more disruptive rebel activities. However, just two months later, we experienced our fourth and most traumatic robbery in our home one evening. After spending a sleepless night waiting for daylight, we packed a suitcase and drove to Bujumbura. We were relaying our story to our leader, Bishop Buconyori, when a phone call came to his office. It was the vice-governor of Gitega Province.

"I hear that Dr. Ogden has left Kibuye. What can we do to get him to return?" He was concerned because I was the only doctor in the region at the time.

"We cannot allow him and his wife to return unless you send security," the bishop answered. Subsequently, they did that. The government established a police post near our house on the mission compound. No more worries at night as to whether the watchman is calling me to the hospital for an emergency C-section, or is it armed robbers again? But sending those soldiers to guard us would come later. At this point, we were about ready to get a plane for Seattle. Bishop Buconyori sat us down for a kindly talk.

"Please don't go back home; stay nearby. I have something for you to do in Kenya." He then explained that he would like Carol to teach a class on Free Methodist History at the FM Bible School in Kericho, adding, "I was scheduled to teach it, but I'm not able to go." He then handed Carol the text book.

We agreed and flew to Nairobi in April 2003, borrowed a car from missionary friends Jim and Martha Kirkpatrick, and drove to Kericho, two hundred miles northwest of Nairobi. We stayed for two weeks, using the home of missionaries who were on furlough. It was a good experience to work with pastors in another African nation, and very helpful that they spoke English well.

God's Help with Car Troubles

Besides the time mentioned earlier in this chapter when "an angel" helped us change a tire with no jack, we experienced other vehicle rescues for which we give God all the praise. One time we had our Toyota van serviced in Bujumbura; then headed up the 5000 foot climb on our way home to Kibuye. Our visiting dental team was with us, Drs. Hodges and Davenport, with their wives as dental assistants. When we reached the top of the escarpment, steam was hissing out of the hood.

Apparently the mechanic had not gotten the radiator cap on correctly. It had fallen off and was nowhere to be found. There happened to be a public water faucet nearby. We let the engine cool and added water, pouring with a coffee pot we happened to have on board. Looking around we found in the ditch a corn cob to act as a radiator cap. The dentists looked in their kits to

114

find floss for tying the corn cob in place. We took extra water in a bucket we had and refilled the radiator again along the road. We bought a new radiator cap at the next town and we made it home OK.

Years earlier, on our way home to Kibuye from Gitega our Ford Bronco burst a large hole in the radiator hose. We lost the fluid, and the engine overheated. There was a stream nearby, but we only had an empty Coke bottle to fill with water. This required many trips to the stream to even half fill the radiator. We tied a rag around the offending hose and drove slowly home. Fortunately, it was only a few miles. A replacement hose was found, and the repair was easy. The motor did not suffer harm.

Since Kibogora is far from the capital of Kigali and in 1985 much of the road was not yet paved, getting to and from Kigali in rainy season was sometimes difficult; as the following story shows. We were called to a meeting in Kigali in October, which is rainy season. We drove the small Daihatsu truck, which is not 4-wheel drive, in order to haul back a new portable x-ray unit. We were held up seven hours in a construction zone in the mountains. We waited in the sun. We drank all the water in the thermos and what pop we had. We had four Africans with us on the truck, so the drinks didn't last very long.

The truck would lose power which could mean water in the fuel or a coil going out. Darkness fell as we limped along at 10 mph. Local people walking along the road tried to help us up a muddy hill but failed. The Lord kept our truck running as we made a 25-mile detour through much mud and several stream crossings.

We got home to Kibogora at 10:00 PM, fifteen hours after we had left Butare just 100 miles behind us. Fortunately the rain had stopped during this marathon. Once again, God proved himself protector and provider.

When I married Carol she came with a Nissan Patrol (4WD jeep) in the deal. That was very good; however, we had some trouble on a long journey from Bujumbura to Kibogora. Shortly after leaving war-torn Burundi and climbing the mountains into Rwanda, the shackle on the right front wheel support broke, allowing the wheel to rub under the fender.

We were miles from any mechanical assistance with an undriveable vehicle. With no cell phones in those days, what were we to do? While I pondered the situation, Carol noted all the positive things about this breakdown, "We are no longer in rebel held territory; it isn't raining; it isn't dark; and I see a hut over there where we can inquire about using their outhouse."

In the back of the vehicle I found a small 2x4. I got out the jack and raised the wheel. I was then able to put the 2x4 between the axle and the chassis, binding it in place with my trusty nylon tow strap. This kept the wheel from rubbing and we were able to slowly drive to the nearest town of Cyangugu, approximately 15 miles ahead. We stopped twice to tighten the tow strap on the block of wood.

I stopped at the only restaurant in town to use the telephone, wondering who I was going to call. Just then, a European man I scarcely knew stepped up and asked if I was having trouble. He recognized me and probably thought *Doctors don't usually wear coveralls*.

I explained our situation and he quickly said, "I think our mechanic can help you. Follow me". This kind man led us to the compound of a Dutch aid agency. His wife welcomed us into their home, offering a place to rest and giving us refreshments for our three-hour wait. We were five people in all and greatly appreciated her hospitality.

Finally, the mechanic was finished and only charged us $20, saying he was happy to help because I had operated on his father. We made it on to Kibogora, another one and a half hour drive, pulling in at dark, tired but glad to have made it home that same day. We thanked God for helping us once again in dire circumstances.

Chapter 10
FINAL YEARS OF SERVICE

The civil war in Burundi lasted twelve years, from 1993-2005. Even though we were not targets in this war, there were enough disturbing activities to keep us vigilant and ready to flee at a moment's notice. Road blocks halted cars while rebel soldiers demanded money in order to pass. Patients came to the hospital with gunshot or stab wounds. Curfews made it impossible to drive after dark, which is fine unless an emergency would arise. We kept working despite these uncertainties, and the underlying tension felt by our national colleagues. Looking back now, it's remarkable that we were able to recruit small teams to join us during these turbulent times. God was certainly with us!

Since we were mainly living at Kibogora from 1997-2000 some of our work teams came to help us there, and some of *these* were able to go to Kibuye also.

In December 1999 Francine Walls came to document our work using her professional photography skills, then developing a script for a slide show (before electronic means). During our Home Assignment in 2000 we used this presentation over and over as we traveled to churches and camps in the US and Canada.

Mary Norris Larson and her daughter Celeste visited at Christmastime that year. They blessed all the missionaries at Kibogora with Christmas gifts, and helped us "see in" the new millennium.

Another Christmas we had Carol's brother, Chuck (and Nancy) with us. Other relatives who made the long trip to Africa to visit us in our final years there include grandson Matthew Ogden; Carol's parents, Lyle & Elsie Watson; her brother Larry (and Carolyn) Watson; her nephew Nathan Watson; and my sister Myrtle Moller.

Myrtle and her husband, Don, made a visit for a month in 2000 after we had made the move from Kibogora to Kibuye. Myrtle was a retired nurse who had wanted for a long time to go help her surgeon brother in Africa. Occasionally we would hear gunfire, but it was far away.

One day during their time with us Myrt and Don heard gunfire very close to the mission. It so happened that Carol and I were gone all day visiting patients at Muyebe Dispensary. Myrt and Don were in two different places on the mission compound at the time and decided to get together at the house so they "could be killed together". Fortunately, nothing happened but it did give them a fright and a good story to tell later back home.

BIG KNIFE "Kibugita"

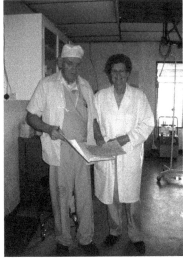

FO with sister Myrtle
Moller, RN, 2009

Carol & FO dressed for
church. 2008

Dr Frank and Carol Ogden
with Bishop Elie Buconyori

Frank & Carol Ogden with Bishop Elie Buconyori.
early 2000's

The Mollers had timed their visit so that we four could leave together as we made our way homeward for Home Assignment, using an Around the World ticket. We took three weeks to reach Seattle by going east from Africa, staying with friends in Mauritius, Taipei, Kaohsiung, Hong Kong, and Osaka.

We were welcomed home in Seattle by family and friends very glad that we had not been shot, when we were robbed those times. We gladly entered the deputation trail, traveling to churches and camps telling people how God was working through us in Central Africa. Often in these presentations I quoted the last part of Psalm 40:3, "Now many will hear the glorious things He has done for me, and stand in awe before the Lord, and put their trust in Him." Truly, God has helped us in marvelous ways to share the Good News of salvation to our people in Rwanda and Burundi. At this writing the Free Methodist Church of Burundi, of which we have been a small part, numbers 179,600+ members and Rwanda has 136,500+. Each of these far exceeds the membership of our combined FM churches in the USA & Canada.

Later in the year 2000 we returned to Africa, completing our around-the-world trip. It was my third time to use this special type of ticket, but the first for Carol. We still had another five years of service before our official retirement in June 2005.

Frank Ogden School of Medicine (FOSM)

In 2004 Bishop Dr. Elie Buconyori, president of Hope Africa University, called Carol and me into his office to tell us that the university was starting a Health Science Program, including a medical school. He said it was requested by the president of the republic due to the lack of physicians in Burundi. The thought of this four-year-old university starting a medical school was amazing enough, but I was speechless when he continued, "Would it be OK to name it *The Frank Ogden School of Medicine?*" He went on to say that during my many years of service I kept coming back to Burundi, even during difficult times to serve at Kibuye, most of the time as the only doctor. "We don't want people to forget your sacrifice."

FO at Hope Africa University, Bujumbura, Burundi

FO with medical students, 2010

Of course when my tongue would respond I agreed, and then advised that they begin small, admitting only a handful of students. Dr. Elie smiled at me and replied, "We have already started classes with a group of 14 students, the brightest and best in science from secondary school". This illustrates the vision of HAU's first president, the late Rev. Dr. Elie Buconyori, who held a PhD in Higher Education from Trinity International University in Illinois. The development of this university is an extraordinary testament to God's goodness. See haufriends.org

The new Medical School began as a four-year undergraduate program followed by three years of medical courses to reach the MD degree. The undergraduate course has since been shortened to three years. The first class graduated on December 21, 2012. It was an honor to attend this first graduation ceremony.

BIG KNIFE "Kibugita"

1st class of students from Frank Ogden
School of Medicine, 2010

Medical students with Dr Faustin Idumbo

FO at Frank Ogden School of Medicine graduation, 2012

When we were home in the US Carol and I later served on a sub-committee of Friends of HAU to raise funds for the development of this new Frank Ogden School of Medicine (FOSM). With my name on it, of course I wanted to see it succeed. Norm Edwards was our chairman and David Goodnight offered us a meeting room at his law firm in downtown Seattle. God blessed our efforts as we raised awareness and funds, and recruited professors to go share their expertise for a month or a term.

First Medical Students

Two of my students of that first class came to talk with me about further study. They had shown particular aptitude doing surgery with me.

Alliance Niyukuri sought me out at home.

"Doctor, I would very much like to go on into surgery training. I want to be a surgeon like you in order to serve my people. I want to work here at Kibuye." I was glad to hear this.

"Okay!" I replied. "Let's make some contacts. Maybe we can get you a position with PAACS – Pan Africa Academy of Christian Surgeons." I knew they had residency programs in a number of Christian hospitals in Africa. I thought that Alliance's ability in surgery, coupled with his fluency in English, French, and other languages would help him to be accepted, even though coming from a brand new medical school.

"I will be happy to recommend you to PAACS," I said. Knowing that he lacked funds to go to another country for five years of surgery training, I contacted MedSend – a branch of the Christian Medical Dental Association – to get a needed scholarship. I knew that they had recently started offering assistance to graduates of medical schools in Africa in order for them to remain in Africa for surgical training. (Many who trained abroad–in Europe or North America–never returned to serve their own people).

Alliance was accepted by PAACS and assigned to Bongolo Hospital in French-speaking Gabon. He was also accepted by MedSend for scholarship. PAACS advised Alliance, "Don't go to Gabon, leaving your fiancé in Burundi for five years. It is better to marry her and take her with you." Alliance did just that – he and Cynthia got married, then made the big move to Gabon together.

After completing his PAACS residency, Dr. Alliance returned with Cynthia (and two daughters by now) to Burundi and joined the surgical staff at Kibuye. At this writing he and his family are in Malawi as he trains to become a pediatric surgeon.

Then there was Isaac Mubezi. "What will you do when you return to Uganda?" I asked him one day. I knew that he, like Alliance, was interested in surgical training.

"I am contacting a hospital in Kampala for a three-year training program in general surgery," he replied. "Would you be able to write a recommendation for me?"

"I will be happy to make such a recommendation," I said. "How will you finance living and training in Kampala?"

"There is some salary, and some ability for moonlighting to make it."

Isaac was accepted in the program in Kampala. He then graduated from FOSM and married Rachel Jacobs – who had been a professor in the Education department at HAU. He completed his surgical residency and has now moved to his home area in Uganda. Isaac and Rachel (with their three children) are building a fine Christian hospital. Hope and Healing Center is flourishing in a rural area of Uganda that lacks such medical and surgical service. See Something Deeper Ministries.org

Dr. Alliance Niyukuri   Dr. Isaac Mubezi at Hope &
                            Healing Center, Uganda

American Medical Students

From time to time medical students from the US would come for a month to help and learn at one of our mission hospitals. To name them all would be impossible; however, during our final years of service Carol and I especially remember four of these young people.

Nathan Thompson was actually born at Kibuye (son of missionaries Nate and Pris Thompson). He was thrilled to return to his birthplace as an adult studying medicine. I enjoyed teaching him how to do C-Sections and many other operations in both Kibogora and Kibuye. Subsequently, Nathan earned his MD and is in family practice in Redmond, Oregon.

Michele Gray came to Kibogora twice; the first time as a medical student in 2001, and the second as a resident the following year. She later qualified in OBGyn and has been in active practice in St. Joseph, Michigan. (Michele and her husband, Tim Ashton, PA filled in for me at Kibuye for three weeks in 2009).

Jennifer Parish (Ceserta) from Washington State also came to Kibogora in 2001, along with her parents Lee and Joyce. They pitched in to help in many ways. Jennifer is now a pediatrician, working in a faith based practice.

There's a story behind the young man who helped us for two months later that year. While on home assignment, traveling to churches speaking about the work in Africa, we were sometimes given gifts or free services. Lodging in a church members' home was common in those days. One time we were staying with the family of Dr. Mike Benedick, a dentist.

"Would you like me to fix your teeth while you're here in Southern Idaho?" Dr. Benedick asked.

"That would certainly be nice," I replied. The next day we went with our host to his dental clinic where he gave free care to Carol and me. What a wonderful gift. Then Mike asked,

"Would it be possible for my son, Dan, to make a visit to Africa to observe and assist you there? He is soon to graduate from college and plans to go into medicine."

That is too soon I thought to myself as I like to have students who are in their third or fourth year of medical school to come to Africa to help and learn from me, not those just hoping for a career in medicine. However, after what this kind dentist did for us I could not refuse.

We were able to meet Dan and could see that he was a fine young man and the first baseman on the

Northwest Nazarene University baseball team. We made the arrangements and Dan Benedick came and worked with me that summer. He proved to be very good with his hands and a quick learner. Perhaps my recommendation helped him get accepted at Loma Linda University School of Medicine.

There's more to this story. After getting his MD Dan took a family practice residency, married a fine Christian lady named Kristina, and moved his little family to the Hospital Vozandes del Oriente at Shell Mera, Ecuador. The Benedicks, under the scholarship of World Medical Mission served here at the edge of the Amazon jungle for two years.

During that period, in 2011, Carol and I took a vacation to Ecuador where we stayed a few days in the home of the Benedicks. Kristina had recently given birth to their third child. It was rewarding to see Dr. Dan serving in a mission hospital. I even got to assist in one operation.

Volunteer Teams

As mentioned earlier, our official retirement as career missionaries with FM World Missions occurred in June of 2005. We now had Dr. Mukenga as medical director, and Kibuye Hope Hospital (KHH) was now part of the Frank Ogden School of Medicine (FOSM). However, this did not mean "rocking chair retirement" as we remained active for another seven years–speaking in various churches and camps, raising funds for the medical school, and leading teams back to Kibuye.

Interspersing our volunteer trips to Africa with speaking engagements proved to be a good rhythm for Carol and me in semi-retirement. Many of the assignments were at summer camps; one at Kakabeka Falls, Ontario. This camp was on a river that flows into Lake Superior. We have a nice memory of floating on inner tubes down the river one warm afternoon with some twenty other campers. Then it was time to head back to Kibuye.

Each time we were packing up in the US to return to Central Africa we took as many medical supplies in our luggage as possible. We also took people with us to share their various gifts, and to catch the vision of what God was doing in another part of the world.

Some of the friends who worked with us for short periods between 1998 and 2012 include Gerry & Della Rockhill (teaching solar cooking and doing general maintenance); Gary Hirayama and Jeff Yerger (handymen who repaired many things); and Sara Moorman and her son Dan. As a medical student, Dan was eager to scrub with me in surgery. Sara did a technical measurement of the property at Kibuye.

One team who accompanied us in 2008 was composed of the Hamilton Family–Doug and Karen, sons Andrew and Aaron, and Karen's mother Audrey Thorsen; plus my young cousin, Sandi Reimer (Kruger) who was interested in medicine. Following them came our friends Gary & Juelle Edwards. Gary made a video which we used to promote the work.

In 2009 we had Bob and Judy O'Brien helping us with maintenance and sewing. During this time a prayer team led by Marti Ensign and Bonnie Brann also came to bless us.

Dr. Mike McGee, ENT surgeon and Dr. J.D. Parkhurst, Urologist came several times when I was away in the States. They and their teams were a great help by "standing in the gap".

Our two-month trip in 2010 was especially eventful. We were preparing for the first class of medical students who would be moving to Kibuye for their clinical training. We completed and furnished the 16-bed dormitory to house the students. Dr. Doug Trotter, with his wife Kathy, took a week from their one-year service at Kijabe Hospital, Kenya, to come help me right at that time. He was such an encouragement as we launched the very first clinical program for the Frank Ogden School of Medicine. See Appendix 2 for more details of this historic event.

A team of four friends with varying skills arrived after the Trotters left–Paul and Linda Busic, Elaine Williamson and Dr. Jerry Rusher. Paul helped me on mechanical and electrical issues. The two of us worked together in the ditch hooking up the cable to the new maternity ward being built. Linda sewed surgical drapes and gowns and much more. Elaine, a medical technologist had worked at Kibuye years before. This time she returned to upgrade our laboratory services. Jerry was a huge help in training the medical students. (He had years of experience in working in hospitals in Haiti and South Africa.) I will say more about Jerry later in this chapter.

During those months we also built a quadriplex to house the new long-term medical team who was coming to serve after us. The last of our working trips was November 2012 to January 2013. It was good to see that the hospital was able to continue through these difficult years of continuing civil unrest. Three of our armed robberies occurred during these short-terms of service.

Dr. Patricia Rees, surgeon, was also helpful in training medical students. Her first visit was in the fall of 2011, and she came again with her husband Fenton, an electrical engineer who repaired equipment and made an assessment of the electrical systems. (He later returned as a team member of Engineering Ministries International (EMI).

In January 2012 Drs. Joel and Janette Miller, our missionary colleagues based in Bujumbura, moved upcountry for a period, to work with the medical students they had already taught in the classroom at HAU. They were rewarded by seeing their students now applying theory to practice by caring for actual patients.

Steve Bressler with Medical Teams International (MTI) came to do a technical review of the water and power systems. Dr. Sarah Crawford, ER doc helped us that same year.

The team from Seattle First Church contributed their gifts of service in early 2012: Pastor Mark Abbott held conferences for pastors in both Burundi and Rwanda. Ron Haight recorded African music performed by numerous singers on various traditional instruments. He and others laid new floor tile in the second Operating Room at Kibuye. Gordon and Sara Moorman assisted in many ways, as did Dr. Andrew Rice and his wife Susan; and Dr. Len and Marti Ensign. This team witnessed a miracle when a customs official changed his mind about charging duty for essential medical supplies, after we had prayed.

Bob Schill from Missionary TECH Team came to draw up plans for future expansion of the hospital complex. Midwife Karen Hayes with husband Scott Nordquist, anesthesiologist, served for several months. Dermatologist friend Craig Maddox came with his family for a month during our final Christmas in Africa.

All these folks helped us in various ways and we are so grateful. To list all our helpers during these years would be difficult, but I must give special mention to my dear friend Dr. Jerry Rusher.

Jerry was my best helper, especially in teaching the medical students when they came for their clinical work at Kibuye Hope Hospital.

It was great to see how he would make a differential diagnosis (a list of various things that might be going on) following a student's presentation of a patient. With five or six students gathered around him at the bedside (or in the conference room) Jerry would show the students how certain symptoms ruled in or ruled out each diagnosis to the point of having one definitive diagnosis to work on. He would then ask one of the students to propose a treatment plan and see if the group would agree with it. Or he might propose a better plan, taking into consideration our limitation on the medicines available in our pharmacy, or which could be obtained elsewhere in the country.

Sometimes the diagnosis was not made initially; so Jerry would study that evening, consulting medical books, or just thinking about the situation in order to assist in the diagnosis. Then he would discuss his find-ings with the students the next day, as well as evaluate any changes that had occurred in the patient. By then lab results might be available. When a particularly inter-esting case appeared, Jerry would make sure that other students beyond his small group had the opportunity to examine the patient (when relevant) and understand the treatment. His compassionate handling of each patient was also remarkable.

The students and Dr. Jerry would follow the progress of their patients together in subsequent days, making changes as necessary. Sometimes it took several days to figure out the patient's diagnosis and optimal treatment. Each student was urged to participate. On maternity problems he was also very good at explaining things in the progress of labor, and possible need for Cesarean section or vacuum extraction.

It is noteworthy that in 2010 Jerry continued teaching medical students for two more months after others on the team had left. He was then alone in the big mission house, so in the evenings he would spend time with the medical students (playing games, singing hymns, etc.), which further strengthened his bond with them.

Jerry returned to Kibuye the next year, serving for five months, and again in 2012. This time he brought his new wife, a retired nurse. Lilly Ann and Jerry had both lost their spouses to cancer. Carol and I introduced this fine couple to each other, and it has been won-derful watching them work together. It happened like this. We had arranged to meet Dr. Pat Rees at Denny's Restaurant near our place in Everett to discuss her upcoming month of service at Kibuye. (Pat, a surgeon, would be filling in when I couldn't be there.) She called me the day before our appointment.

"Would it be okay if a retired nurse friend would go with me to Burundi? I will bring her to the restaurant to meet you and talk about the trip."

"Sure," I replied," bring her along."

That is how Carol and I met Lilly Ann Haugo. We could see her vibrant Christian character and passion for medical missions. It seemed that Pat and Lilly Ann would make a great team.

As we left the restaurant Carol said to me, "That Lilly Ann is the just the one for Jerry!" I readily agreed, and we arranged for them to meet at a dinner in Pat's home once Jerry had returned from Kibuye. After that, the courtship blossomed, and we were not surprised to hear of their engagement a few months later. Lilly Ann called me as Carol and I were making plans to leave for another three months of service at Kibuye.

"When do you get home from Burundi?"

"March first," I said.

"Okay, we will get married March second. You guys *must* be there." At this point, I had not even been asked by Jerry to be the best man. It worked out well. We got home as planned on the first. The rehearsal was on the second, and the wedding was on March third (as it turned out), 2012. This couple, devoted to each other and to medical missions, headed out to Kibuye not long afterwards.

Besides the American doctors mentioned above I am grateful for the African physicians who were involved in this transition period and training of students, particularly, Drs. Prospere, Wilson, Clovis and Faustin.

Chapter 11

KIBUYE TODAY...BURUNDI'S CHRISTIAN MEDICAL CENTER

The seeds sown in Central Africa in 1935 by Rev. J.W. Haley have certainly borne fruit. I have been privileged to be part of the "watering" of that seed but all praise goes to God who really made it happen. I echo the words from Dr. Robert Laws, pioneer missionary to Malawi. After forty-five years of service he said, *"Duty is ours; success is God's. God has been very good to us. It has been His doing. And to Him is due all the praise."*

From my first commitment to Christ at age six, to a fulfilling life of service in Africa, I have felt the guidance of my Lord. I retired in 2005 at age seventy to continue serving part-time until early 2013. I laid aside my scalpel for good when I was 78, knowing the coming team would develop the hospital into a real medical center. They were specialists in general surgery, family practice, emergency room, internal medicine, obstetrics & gynecology, pediatrics & ophthalmology. Heading this group of dedicated Christian servants was Dr. Jason Fader, general surgeon.

How did this team come to be? Five of these doctors had already worked together in another African hospital in Kenya—Tenwek. Most were from the same church and medical school in Ann Arbor, MI. They all felt God had called them as a team to "make a difference" in some developing country. In their own words, *"During our time at Tenwek, we began to eagerly scour the continent for various opportunities, focusing on medical education in areas on the needier side of the African spectrum…In the end all of us decided to apply to World Harvest Mission (now Serge) in order to be sent to Burundi to serve as clinical faculty for the young medical school at Hope Africa University, while providing compassionate care to the poorest of the poor at Kibuye Hope Hospital in the interior of Burundi."* See Word and Deed/McCropders and Serge Mission agency.

First Serge team in 2013

Serge team on a retreat in 2021

Kibuye Hope Hospital when we left in 2013

Kibuye Hope Hospital in 2020

In just eight years we have watched with wonder at the advancement of healthcare at Kibuye Hope Hospital (KHH). I could not have imagined God's working to effect the huge changes in the small hospital where I had served as the only doctor much of the time. KHH is now a medical center with over 300 beds and nearly 20 doctors, half of them Africans. There are also interns, medical students, and nurses in training. The facilities expansion includes two additional operating rooms, a two-story surgical ward, a three-story pediatric building, solar power, and an eye center, just to name a few.

It was an honor for our hospital that a Jewish foundation awarded the Gerson L'Chaim prize of $500,000 to Dr. Fader in 2016. See African Mission Healthcare/ L'Chaim prize.

If this weren't enough KHH is becoming a training facility with PAACS which enables African physicians to train in general surgery *in Africa* for service in their own countries. Our graduates are taking their places at medical facilities around Burundi and beyond. Some are planning to be medical missionaries, following the model of the Serge team.

For all of this I praise the Lord who allowed me a small part in bringing about this fruit as I was "Operating for God in Africa".

EPILOGUE

If I had stayed in the United States practicing surgery for my career instead of going to Central Africa, I would have made a lot more money. However, I would have missed the wonderful life that God has given me. I have found happiness in serving the Lord Jesus Christ—not in driving a Mercedes or living in luxury. He has blessed our investments in order for us to travel extensively, including around the world twice with Maxine and twice with Carol. I have been able to visit 98 countries and territories thus far, so I think to count two more before my days on earth are finished.

FO receiving Humanitarian of the Year award from UW Medicine President Dr. Paul Ramsey, 2011

Now in retirement we are enjoying life in a Christian condominium complex, surrounded by like-minded friends. We are able to spend several winter months in sunny Tucson, Arizona where numbers of both Carol and my close relatives are our neighbors. It pays to serve Christ wherever He leads across the globe.

THE LAST WORD
by Carol Ogden

F rank has always had this joke about having "the last word". While giving presentations about our missionary work we would often be at the podium together—he sharing for a few minutes, then me, back to him and so forth. Typically I would give the concluding remarks, then Frank would lean into the microphone and say "I get the last two words… *Yes, dear*."

This time he has given *me* the privilege of giving the last words in this book. Having joined the exciting life of "Big Knife" later in his life gives me a unique perspective. I've been able to walk with this doctor through his last fifteen years of missionary service and see up close his tender heart for the African people he served.

Working on this book with Frank has given me a new appreciation for the influence of his Godly parents, for the many years of preparation, and for the earlier chapters of his life in Africa with Maxine and their children.

Frank has lived through three periods of civil war in Burundi and Rwanda (one of those with me), during his four-plus decades of involvement in missions. He lost his first wife to cancer before she reached sixty. Yet he says with the hymn writer, "It will be worth it all, when we see Jesus…"

I got to be by his side as Frank received the two biggest honors in this season of his life: birth of the

Frank Ogden School of Medicine, and being awarded "Humanitarian of the Year" by the University Of Washington School Of Medicine.

The first one was when I heard Bishop Buconyori ask Frank if he could name the new medical school after him. "We want future generations to know the name of Frank Ogden, the doctor who kept returning to Burundi to care for the sick, even during times of war." *Wow,* I thought, *what an honor!*

Six years later I was thrilled to meet the first class of medical students as they stepped off the bus with their duffle bags, ready to settle into the dorm at Kibuye and begin clinical work at the hospital. Frank was beginning to see the fruits of his service—here were the doctors of the future who would succeed him. (See full details in Appendix 2.)

It was Dr. Doug Trotter, our friend from Snohomish, Washington who nominated Frank for the Humanitarian Award. We have in our file the letters of recommendation he collected from Dr. Elisee Nahimana and Dr. Georges Ntakiyiruta, from KHH Administrator Japhet Nsanzerugeze and from Bishop Elie Buconyori. A few comments from these African colleagues are worth sharing here.

Dr. Ogden became a model for my life. When I went to university I chose the faculty of medicine…later I continued my studies in surgery…I was very happy to be a surgeon like him.—EN

Dr. F. Ogden is a very good teacher. I remember whenever he was called at any time of the day or night, he would always be there and he would teach you how to do it. I was always amazed by his energy and love for patients. –GN

Dr. Frank Ogden has spent a major part of his life serving Christ and Africans in Africa...While meeting the health needs of the people, Dr. Ogden was always working with the church in order to encourage pastors to meet the spiritual needs of the people...His commitment to serve humanity in general and the people of Burundi in particular was evident during the 12 years of civil war...(he) showed tremendous courage...working day and night treating the sick...During his absence from Burundi he would raise funds...to help pay salaries of local workers and buy medicines...he not only provided equipment and infrastructure, but also supported nationals to get training." –EB

On behalf of the staff of Kibuye Hospital, Busoma, the Station and my own name, let me...express our sincere gratitude for you Doctor and your wife for the love and deep concern you always show to Kibuye Hospital and for the Burundi Free Methodidst Church...—JN

Shying away from these accolades, Frank feels blessed to have had a part in building God's Kingdom in Central Africa through medicine and surgery. He gives all the glory to God saying, "It was worth it all."

Appendix 1
HEROES OF THE FAITH

W e hope these true stories of seven Christian leaders we knew in Africa will encourage you in your faith. We told some of these testimonies in churches and camps while making presentations on our deputation ministry; others were published in various magazines.

Ananiya Emedi
By Dr. Frank Ogden, MD.
October 2003

"There's nothing more we can do for him", I said sadly. "Let us have a prayer meeting by his bed." This was 1971, and the place was Kibuye Hospital, Burundi. The man on his death bed was Pastor Ananiya Emedi. He had severe diabetes and had fallen ill with the disease, because no insulin was available.

Some 50 years earlier, Ananiya was born in Congo, where he grew up and began his ministry. Later he moved to neighboring Burundi, where he planted several churches with members totaling more than 2,000 persons. One day he approached the leaders of the Burundi Free Methodist Church, and asked if his churches could join their denomination. Mergers of this sort are not always helpful, but in this case, Pastor

Ananiya's group of Christians proved to be a wonderful addition to the already established FMC of Burundi.

Over the next 45 years Ananiya established forty churches in the Ruzizi River valley, which begins near Bujumbura along the shores of Lake Tanganyika extending up into the mountains of Burundi. This humble man of God was small in stature but a giant in faith. He never learned to drive a car; he reached all of his preaching points on foot, bicycle or taxi. Often Pastor Ananiya would be returning home after dark in areas frequented by bandits, or in torrential rains. His untiring work spanned several wars in Burundi, but he never faltered. He suffered frequent bouts of malaria and had heart disease; then later, cataracts slowed him down, yet his spirit was always refreshing to see.

As the hospital staff and missionaries gathered around the pastor's bedside that day, they prayed that God would spare his servant; and that is exactly what He chose to do. A miracle happened that day and Pastor Ananiya got up and left the hospital a few days later. The Lord did not cure the diabetes, but he allowed this man to continue serving him another thirty+ years to accomplish more things for the kingdom of God.

In 2002 this great warrior for the Lord in Central Africa finally went to his Heavenly reward. We regret his passing, but we realize he can now rest at the feet of Jesus–the one he served so well for so long.

Pastor Ananiya's influence is felt far and near, for the Ruzizi region in which he labored now has Free Methodist members numbering over 40,000, organized into seven districts. What a great harvest of souls was initiated by this very dedicated man over a span of nearly fifty years. Even during his fifteen years following retirement, this brother continued to be an inspiration to those of us still serving our church in active ministry.

God has not found many of the caliber of Ananiya Emedi to spread the Gospel in Central Africa like this man, but many of us can have a part in the Kingdom by helping people both physically and spiritually. We can take courage from knowing how God has used this man even though afflicted with severe diabetes.

Binyoni's Last Words
As told to Frank Ogden by Marti Ensign

In 1972 a Hutu attempt to unseat the Tutsi government in Burundi failed, and terrible reprisals followed. Educated Hutus were hunted and killed. A teacher of the Evangelical Friends Church named Binyoni was taken. With a Caterpillar the authorities had dug a large trench near Gitega. They lined up their victims to shoot them. They would fall into the trench, then be covered by the Cat dead or alive. When Binyoni was about to be shot, he asked if he might sing a song first. The wish was granted, and he sang the hymn "Jesus, I Come" whose final verse says,

> *Out of the fear and dread of the tomb,*
> *Jesus, I come, Jesus, I come;*
>
> *Into the joy and light of Thy home, Jesus,*
> *I come to Thee;*

*Out of the depths of ruin untold, Into the
peace of Thy sheltering fold,*

*Ever Thy glorious face to behold, Jesus,
I come to Thee.*

The soldiers then carried out their orders as directed.
A lieutenant who was on the scene was so moved by this
testimony–given in this crucial situation–that he came
to the Christian Book Store in Gitega to tell missionary
Esther Choate this amazing story. In this way many of
us missionaries heard this wonderful testimony of a
believer just before being killed. Our colleague, Marti
Ensign is a gifted story-teller and has told of Binyoni's
dying words far and wide. We are not sure of the heart
response of that soldier.

Eliezar Ndibadibe
By Frank Ogden

A young boy was herding the family's goats by the
Kibuye Free Methodist Church (FMC). He was curious
about what was being preached, so he listened at the
window. He heard the Good News of the Gospel of
Christ and became a true follower of the Lord. The
boy's family was poor and he was not able to attend
secondary school, so he had only six years of education
which was taught in Kirundi.

However, the church leaders recognized Eliezar
Ndibadibe's zeal and leadership ability. He became
a pastor and then the superintendent of the Kibuye
District of the FMC. I cared for him in his later years.

By then he had developed diabetes, but in those years we had insulin and other diabetic medications. He has now gone on to Glory after serving the church for more than 50 years.

Two of Pastor Ndibadibe's sons have served at Kibuye: Duk as my anesthetist for many years, and Pamphil as manager of the mission station workers.

Andre Barutwanayo
By Frank Ogden

Before the civil war began in Burundi in 1993, Andre Barutwanayo was a bi-vocational pastor. For four days of the week he worked for me at Kibuye Hospital– in fact, I trained him first as an Operating Room technician; later he expanded into general nursing. On the weekends Andre rode his bicycle twenty-five miles to his church, teaching on Saturdays, and preaching on Sundays. His humble nature and untiring zeal brought a lot of fruit for the Lord.

Then came the war and Andre, fearing for his life, fled into Tanzania, as did many of our staff. By this time he was married and had two young children. "Those were terrible times", he recalls. "First we walked for two days to the border. Then at the river we got into a boat to cross over, but there was shooting all around us. Finally we jumped in the river, and God helped us make it to the Tanzanian shore to safety."

For seven years Andre and his family lived in a two-room thatched hut with a tarp over the top. Food was scarce and disease was everywhere. Their second child, a boy, died of illness at two years of age, for lack of medical attention. But God was faithful to Andre and his wife Marie Gorett. Both of them found employment at a hospital near the refugee camp, which gave them a small income. Andre became active in the Free Methodist Church which had started in the camp, and soon he was pastoring it.

He wrote to me during those years of displacement and gave me progress reports on the Lord's work. This man of God kept a positive spirit during very difficult times, and trusted God for his future. In 2003 he finally brought his wife and four children back home to Burundi. We gave him work once again at the hospital.

At this same time, other refugees from the same camp in Tanzania had returned to their home area in Burundi. They had become Christians in the camp and knew Pastor Andre; so they asked the superintendent in their area, if they could be a Free Methodist congregation. Because he knew these folks and their circumstances, Andre was appointed as their pastor even though this new congregation is about fifty miles from Kibuye! It was taking him two days by bicycle each way to visit them–while still working at the hospital part time. I decided to buy him a motorcycle to help him get to his church each week. This changed a two-day journey into a two-hour journey. Thus, he could go to his parish for the weekend–doing Bible teaching, and visiting parishioners on Saturday, and preaching on Sunday–then ride his motorcycle back to Kibuye to help me in the hospital on Monday without being exhausted. Andre is a true servant of the Lord.

Testimony of Jason Haonga

As told to Carol Ogden
Jan 2003

Young Jason grew up in Zambia, Africa, near the northern end of Malawi. His people and language were the same as those across the border, so he moved freely between the two countries. Although his father was a nominal Catholic the family never went to church. The children did not know about Sunday School, so there was no religious training for them. Jason says that his parents took him to the witchdoctor whenever he was sick. Christianity had not penetrated far beneath the surface for this family.

As a teenager Jason had one passion–to fight! He would fight anyone and everyone. He soon joined a tough gang that called themselves "The American Gangsters". Jason says about those days, "Everyone was afraid of us, even the police!" He may have gotten into serious trouble with his fighting, but God had his hand on this young man. He managed to finish High School and excelled in English (which would be a great help to him later).

In his late teen years Jason began thinking about the meaning of life and became enamored with a Christian sect (Jehovah's Witness). He studied hard to be a faithful follower. Working his way up into the leadership of this group, he did all he could to satisfy the spiritual longing in his heart. After twenty years with the JW's Jason was reading the Bible on his own one day when a new truth hit him hard. "I discovered that Jesus is God!" He realized he had been following a false teaching and quickly left it.

He joined the nearest church he could find, not knowing anything about it. But the Lord revealed to him in a dream that this was a dead church. "The angels in my dream knew I wanted to know the true God, so they made it clear that I should leave that church." Soon after this dramatic encounter Jason met an evangelist with the Free Methodist Church of Malawi.

"This man taught me the way of Jesus Christ and urged me to go to Bible School. That was in 1997." Jason began his first one-month module at the Free Methodist Bible School (now Great Commission Bible School) in Lilongwe, Malawi; where his excellent English helped him tremendously. He had to leave his wife and children and take a long bus ride to the campus in Malawi's capital city, but he tackled his classes eagerly. "I wanted to learn everything about my new faith, the true faith, since I had wasted many years of my life."

As one of the school requirements Jason was soon planting a church in his home village in Zambia. His class modules at the Bible School were interspersed with periods of caring for this flock and others, as he continued to start churches. The Lord used Jason's leadership skills he had learned years earlier in the JW church to make him an effective Free Methodist pastor. Still, it was difficult to leave his family each time another module came around.

"It meant leaving the cultivation of the fields to study in faraway Lilongwe for a month. But God was with us. He helped my wife to be resourceful and make the food stretch. I had many courses with good professors. Small group Bible studies and fellowship with other students strengthened my faith. I attended fifteen modules over a six-year period and finally in October 2002 I graduated. I am now pastoring three churches whose members are reaching out to others."

God has raised up a powerful servant for the Free Methodist Church in Malawi. He saw the longing in Jason's heart for the true faith, and He revealed Jesus Christ to him. Jason thinks back on those "wasted years", but God is using those experiences to help him deal with others struggling with true faith.

Matthew Hacimana
By Carol Ogden
September 2004

Matthew is a small, quiet man living in rural Burundi. He has an infectious smile and his dark eyes speak love and the kind of understanding that comes through suffering. God's hand has been upon this servant since he was a boy. When he finished the sixth grade Matthew had the opportunity to attend Mweya Bible School for his secondary education. He was a serious student and took special interest in his Science classes. All subjects were taught in French, a big change from grade school, but he adapted well. Like most Mweya students Matthew learned good English too, since his teachers were native English speakers (North American missionaries). In fact, he especially excelled in this subject.

It was no surprise that after graduation Matthew became a favorite interpreter for visiting work teams and short term missionaries to the Kibuye area of Burundi. Later, he got a job at Kibuye Mission Hospital as a technician in the Operating Room. He was trained on the job and learned quickly. Soon he was handing instruments to the doctor during surgery, or dressing wounds on patients.

Matthew was also growing in his spiritual life. As a born-again believer he trusted God for a Christian wife and the Lord brought Marguerite into his life. They were married and began a family. They built a home within a five-minute walk of the hospital and their church. Marguerite began teaching school in a neighboring district, a walk of some thirty minutes. All was going well for this family until the 1993 civil uprising in Burundi. This war affected everyone in some way.

As the war smoldered on year after year, suddenly one day Matthew was falsely accused of having killed a number of people. He did not know the victims nor the woman who was accusing him! Stunned and hurt by this lie, Matthew went quietly off to prison, trusting the Lord to help him in an unjust system, awaiting a trial which never came. For nearly three years he endured the shame and deprivations of a crude prison system. However, during a visit by friends he told them, "I praise God because many prisoners are beaten here, but the guards have never touched me."

Finally Matthew was released with no charges and sent home to his wife and children. What a happy day for everyone! When Sunday came he was given time in the pulpit to praise God for his deliverance. He returned to his work at the hospital, thankful that his job remained open for him.

Soon after this, Matthew felt God calling him to pastoral ministry, so after some preparation he was ordained in 2002. He is now (2004) a bi-vocational pastor, working in the Operating Room Monday through Friday, and then on Sunday (and sometimes Saturday) he goes to his church to shepherd his flock and guide them spiritually. We were able to get him a motorcycle to make that journey easier. It was to Matthew's church that we were going when we had to be late, as both he and Dr. Frank were called to the hospital to do a C-section. (See chapter 9). Matthew has led a consistent life of obedience to the Lord.

Matthew Hacimana with FO

Eraste Mukenga
By Carol Ogden
October 2004

Dr. Eraste Mukenga stood in front of the hospital entrance and gazed around him in amazement. "Am I really here?" he wondered. "Thank you, Lord, for bringing me safely home." His mind wandered back to the last time he had been at Kibuye. This brick wall and these metal gates weren't here. Security hadn't been such an issue then. A lot had happened since he went off to medical school fourteen years before.

Mukenga had received a scholarship from the Free Methodist Mission and Church of Burundi to study medicine in Madagascar, an island country off the east coast of Africa. He moved there with his wife, Charlotte and two small children, and soon plunged into six hard years of study. He was an eager student, always keeping his goal in focus: to return home to Burundi and work as a physician at Kibuye Hospital. Mukenga had grown up near Kibuye and had admired the missionary doctors and nurses who came to serve over the years. Many African nurses and midwives were trained and employed there, but so far no Burundian Free Methodist doctor had risen from the ranks.

As an earnest Christian and loyal member of the Free Methodist Church, Mukenga prayed that he might be the one to complete his medical studies and step into the gap of national leadership at Kibuye Hospital. These were his thoughts as he began medical school. He would never have guessed it would take him fourteen years to realize his goal! If he had known the perils that lay along his path, he may have faltered. But God had his hand on Eraste and was working out his plans for him all along.

It was a happy day in 1993 when Mukenga obtained his medical degree and made plans to return to Burundi with his family. But before their travel arrangements were complete a terrible civil war erupted and Burundi fell into a state of chaos. This was no time to return; in fact thousands were fleeing Burundi. Mukenga turned to his church leaders and missionary friends, asking where he should go. They advised the Mukengas to move to Rwanda, northern neighbor to Burundi, where Eraste could begin to work at Kibogora, sister hospital to Kibuye. Dr. Al Snyder and other missionary doctors helped him get started in his new vocation. He eagerly began learning surgical techniques, since his medical training did not give him much practice in this area.

However, some six months after his arrival in Rwanda, the Mukengas had to leave again, this time fleeing for their lives with many Kibogora personnel. Even the missionary staff had to be evacuated. This was the Rwanda genocide of 1994. In the midst of this huge tragedy God had a new place of service for Dr. Mukenga. He began practicing his new skills at Kibuye's other sister hospital, Nundu, in Zaire (now Democratic Republic Congo). He was even farther from his Burundi homeland, but Eraste and Charlotte prayed every day for the civil wars to end, so they and all the other refugees could return home.

God answered their prayer but not right away. Their homeward journey was far from finished. After less than a year at Nundu Hospital, the Mukenga family had to flee again because of war in Zaire. This time they crowded onto the deck of a forty foot boat with about two hundred other people, and crossed Lake

Tanganyika to their third country of refuge, Tanzania. This was a dangerous crossing in the best of times on a boat that size with so many people. The sounds of gun fire around them was no help in this frightening situation. But the Lord was with them, and the boat made it safely to the other shore.

This time there was no Free Methodist hospital to welcome the Mukenga family, so they settled into the dismal life of survival in a refugee camp. It was difficult to get enough food and they lived in a very crude dwelling, but God was with Eraste and Charlotte. Soon he was busy full time treating the sick and injured in the camp.

One year came and went, then two. The family began wondering if things would ever get back to normal. They were longing to return home to Burundi. More than once, rebel soldiers sneaked into the camp and killed people. One of Eraste's physician colleagues was the target of one such raid. He feared he might be next. He sent letters to missionary friends and church leaders, pleading for assistance to help them repatriate.

Finally, after five long years of subsistence level survival and fearing for his life in the Tanzanian refugee camp, Dr. Mukenga got word that Burundi was stable enough for them to return home. What a joyous day! Missionaries Jim & Barbara Stillman were instrumental in passing along funds, so this family could leave and get transport to neighboring Burundi. They left quietly one night, and due to the danger, could not say a word of farewell to their friends and neighbors in the camp. It was a bitter sweet time.

Now it was January 2002. As Dr. Mukenga stood looking at Kibuye Hospital, he was overwhelmed with gratitude to God for bringing him safely back home and for looking after his family. During these fourteen years away, two more precious children had joined the family. One of his teenage sons had decided to study medicine. They had been able to find Free Methodists to worship with as they literally moved "all around Burundi", from Rwanda, to Zaire to Tanzania. He was tired of wandering and ready to settle in and work with missionary Frank Ogden, MD, Kibuye's long-time surgeon. Yes, indeed, God is good.

Update 1: At the time this article was written (2004), Dr. Mukenga was serving as the only doctor at Kibuye Hospital, Burundi. Charlotte works in the business office. Due to continued insecurity in the region Dr. Ogden has only been able to visit twice for several weeks at a time. He plans on returning again in 2005. The Mukengas have experienced a number of armed robberies at their Kibuye home so are now living in the nearby town of Gitega, commuting to Kibuye each day.

Update 2: In June of 2005 Dr. Ogden and his wife Carol retired from active missionary service. In a ceremony in the church Dr. Mukenga took over as Medical Director of Kibuye Hospital. He had commissioned a wood carved plaque to be made which depicted a white man (wearing shoes) placing a huge stethoscope around the neck of an African (barefoot). Many speeches and prayers of thanksgiving were given that day as "Big Knife" gave up the scalpel and reins of leadership. Dr. Frank was nearly seventy years old.

One or two years later Dr. Mukenga & his family moved to Bujumbura to be the personal physician to the president of Burundi, Pierre Nkurunziza. After some years his son told me this was demanding work as "Dad has to travel everywhere the president goes, by vehicle or plane". *That son has himself become a doctor, graduating from the Frank Ogden School of Medicine of Hope Africa University.*

Appendix 2
FROM BOOK-LEARNING
TO HANDS-ON
By Carol Ogden
2010

History was made on March 14, 2010 for Hope Africa University (HAU) and the Frank Ogden School of Medicine in Burundi. It was a usual quiet Sunday afternoon at Kibuye–not much going on. Dinner was finished, dishes cleared and naps taken. Then we heard the bus coming up the hill past our house. It stopped in front of the new eight-room dorm. Children came running to see–something new was about to happen at Kibuye, and six of us Americans were on hand to witness it. The first class of medical students from HAU stepped off the bus with their duffle bags, ready for their first weeks of clinical work at Kibuye Hope Hospital. After a two and one half hour bus ride from the HAU campus in Bujumbura these recent college grads from the city were now going to experience life in rural Burundi for eight weeks.

It was easy to see that these were exceptional students—bright, eager, and ready to embrace the clinical aspect of their training–to put book knowledge into practice. Each had received a BS degree in Human Biology at HAU, and now was in their fifth year of a seven year program. Upon successful completion of requirements these students will emerge as medical doctors, ready to serve their respective African communities. Of the nineteen students who arrived that day eight were women; four were from Rwanda; and two from Uganda. The rest were Burundians. One female student has since married and left the program. We heard a mixture of French, English and Swahili, as they found their rooms and started to settle in. We heard some of their first remarks after getting off the bus: "We finally get to see real patients–touch them, talk to them–not just read about them!"

Dr. Frank Ogden was on hand to work with these medical students, but he wasn't alone. Dr. Faustin Idumbo, staff physician at Kibuye, took part of the group each day to do patient consultations. Dr. Doug Trotter from Snohomish, WA was a big help the first week. He and his wife Kathy were visiting from Kenya, where he was on a one year sabbatical at Kijabe Hospital. Dr. Frank was so grateful for Doug's help in organizing the clinical rotations, and then teaching physical diagnosis to the students. I peeked in to take pictures and saw them practicing on each other, looking in the ears, the eyes and throat. "Say Aaah" was followed by some hearty laughter.

After Dr. Trotter returned to Kenya, veteran missionary Dr. Jerry Rusher arrived to treat patients at Kibuye and help train the students for seven weeks. His experience in South Africa and Haiti helped him in diagnosing tropical diseases. He quickly adapted to Burundi and enjoyed working with the students. (Dr. Rusher will work at Kibuye again with medical students January through June 2011).

The doctors-in-training rotated through outpatient care, maternity, surgery, internal medicine and pediatrics, finally getting hands-on experience with real patients. Their joy in learning and serving was evident on their faces. The hospital was literally overflowing at this time. Ever since the Burundi government promised free medical care to maternity patients and children ages 0-5 the patient load has soared. The staff is stretched, so the medical students can help while learning. I saw them changing dressings, taking blood pressures, helping to put a cast on a patient. Dr. Rusher taught them to take the patient's medical history, before he arrived which saved time with the large numbers of patients to see. The student would communicate with the patient in Kirundi and then explain the symptoms to Dr. Rusher in English. (HAU is a bi-lingual university and students must take intensive English or French, depending on which is their weaker language.)

During this historic first clinical period a special patient was in a private room at Kibuye Hospital. The Rev. Matayo Myiruko, retired pastor and faithful superintendent, had been the first Free Methodist convert in Burundi under J.W. Haley in 1935. Now here he was at age 93 recovering from a broken femur. One day as Dr. Rusher was caring for this patriarch of the Burundi FM Church three medical students–Isaac, Alliance and Christopher–received a special word and blessing from Rev. Myiruko. He challenged them to become doctors who really care about their patients, as well as giving good medical attention. "Like this one" he said, pointing to Dr. Rusher. Then he prayed for them. It was a special moment those three students and their doctor-teacher will never forget. *(Update: Rev. Myiruko died at age 102 in 2020.)*

The motto of HAU is "Facing African Realities" and for these medical trainees that means bringing health and hope to thousands who currently have no access to good medical care. Seeing HAU's first medical students in action assures us that help is on the way. In a few years these men and women will help fulfill that great need. We thank God for each one of them.

Appendix 3
PLANES AND HELICOPTERS

N ow flying planes and helicopters can really be fun; *however*, it is said that it can be hours of boredom punctuated by moments of sheer terror. Here are some stories of my involvement with flying planes in civilian life, and planes and helicopters while a flight surgeon in the US Army.

In 1956 my brothers Milt & Phil Ogden, and good friend, Gene VanBrocklin bought a small plane, a Luscombe 8A for $850. This plane had no radio and no starter. One turned the prop to get a charge from the magneto to start the engine. Of course, you tied the tail wheel while doing that, so the airplane would not run away; or you had someone in the cabin with a foot on the brakes. We flew out of Boeing Field in Seattle with John Galvin as our instructor. When on final approach we would get a green light from the tower in order to land.

After a while, Boeing Field said we could no longer land there, so we moved the plane to Bellevue, just east of Seattle. John taught us many things about flying and landing that plane, as it is prone to ground-looping (if you don't keep the plane straight ahead on landing, it will start turning in a circle with one wing hitting the ground. That is not good.) Fortunately, we did not do that even when landing with a cross-wind.

One day John & I flew to Wenatchee in eastern Washington. It was hot that day, so as we approached Pangborn Field we encountered a "thermal". That is when heat rising from the hot ground interferes with getting the plane to stall and land properly. Thus, we floated down the length of the runway and had to climb back up and around for another approach. This time we did a "forward slip" where you cross controls–ailerons one way and the rudder the other and keeping the nose down until the last moment to make the landing.

For my solo cross-country flight I decided to visit my uncle, Art Carlson, in Madras, Oregon. This involved flying from Bellevue to Portland, up the Columbia River, then up the Deschutes River in Oregon to reach the field at Madras. After I calculated proper time to reach Madras and could not find the airport, I looked for the airport unsuccessfully; so with only thirty minutes of fuel remaining I landed in a stubble wheat field on the Warm Springs Indian Reservation. Nobody was home to help me, so I took off to land near a railroad station on the other side of the river.

I was looking at the idea of landing in a hay field, so I flew over at 100 feet; then dropped down to twenty feet off the ground to look for rocks. But I forgot about the power line, so when I looked up it was right before me. I reasoned that my little 65-horse engine would not get me over the lines, so I decided to go under them. That was fine except there was a fence there, and I hooked my tail wheel on the fence and did a carrier-type landing in a pile of rocks in the other hay field. The plane suffered major damage; but I was not hurt. The door fell off, so I stepped out and walked to the railroad station. The man there used his hand crank phone to call the Redmond station to have them cancel my flight plan, and to call my uncle to come to get me. We later took off the wings and hauled the plane home, and sold it to someone who planned to fix it. I had to pay off my partners, including Phil, who never did take flying lessons.

I then had to borrow another plane to fly to get my license. After a very nervous time with the flight examiner, I took off from Renton Airport out over Lake Washington. I realized that I was using a fuel tank nearly empty, so I reached down to switch to the other tank that was full. I inadvertently switched it to *off*. At 500 feet over the lake the engine died. Fortunately, I recognized the problem and switched to the correct tank, and the engine ran fine.

After graduation from medical school I joined the Army, and while attending flight surgeon school with the Navy in Pensacola, Florida part of the training was to fly the Navy trainer T-34. That was very fun.

Following six months at Pensacola I was stationed at Fort Rucker, Alabama–a training base for Army aviation. I was assigned to the US Army Board for Aviation Accident Research (USABAAR) but also taught in the new Army Flight Surgeon School. My friends there were flight instructors comfortable flying from the co-pilot seat while teaching new pilots, so they let me be the pilot of the de Havilland Beavers or L-19 Cessna that we flew from there. These planes were for instrument flying, so often I donned a hood after takeoff; so I could see nothing but the instruments as we flew all over the Southeast, making instrument approaches to different airports.

One evening while out flying somewhere over Alabama in a Beaver, as we were returning to the base at Fort Rucker fog was forming. Thus we asked for a GCA approach (Ground Control Approach). In that approach the GCA controller on the ground at the base directed us to fly certain compass headings and to begin our descent toward the runway. We were in nothing but white fog, knowing that it might be too dense to make a safe landing. We knew that if that were the case we would have to divert to another airport to land and then, presumably, spend the night.

As we were just about 400 feet off the ground the GCA controller said, "If you do not have visual contact at this time, execute a missed approach." At that moment we saw the lights and the runway directly ahead, so we made a satisfactory landing. Sometimes while speaking in churches I have used this as an illustration of how we may be following God's direction in our lives, not knowing the outcome until on final approach. Then the right path is revealed to us.

I was also privileged to fly helicopters–the H-19 Sikorsky, the H-13 Bell, the H-23 Hiller and the UH-1 HUEY. Helicopters are much different than fixed-wing planes in that when you approach to land a fixed-wing plane you decrease power and maintain adequate air speed not to stall the plane until ready to touch down. In helicopters you add power and kill off the air speed in order to come to a hover; then set it on the ground. I sometimes at first used up a lot of the practice field getting to a hover for proper landing.

Since I was planning to go into surgery after my Army days, I was allowed to attend the American

College of Surgeons meeting in Chicago. Cliff Carlberg and I flew in an Army L-19 to DuPage County Airport near Chicago, and I attended that very large meeting. When ready to go back to Ft. Rucker it was sixteen degrees below zero with snow on the ground. They heated the engine for us, and we took off and climbed to 9,500 feet on our way to Warsaw, Indiana in order to visit Dr. Lamson, the head of our Free Methodist Mission. I was a missionary candidate at that time. The engine started to sputter and below us were snow-covered fields and a freeway with many cars. Cliff leaned the fuel mixture, as it was too rich at that altitude and so cold. It ran very well after that. Another good lesson about flying.

After my army days ended in 1965, I was a resident in general surgery at Virginia Mason Hospital in Seattle. I joined the Evergreen Flying Club, which had a Taylorcraft, a Maule, and a Cessna 182. A notable journey with the 182 was flying to Banff National Park, Alberta, Canada. We flew up around the Columbia Icefields for a close look at the glaciers. I flew with Maxine, Billie, Wesley and Ronda as a small baby. Brother-in-law, Jerry Reed and his family drove our car to Banff; so we had ground transport while camping at Banff. A bear visited our camp one day.

On the return to Seattle we flew to Calgary for fuel then headed south to Lethbridge. The radio stopped working, so I landed in Lethbridge to get it fixed. They said, "No radio repair service here. You must go to Calgary."

"I don't want to go back to Calgary. I just came from there."

He said, "Well! You can follow the highway to Great Falls, Montana."

I agreed, but when we took off the radio worked again (so we didn't follow that plan). There was a thunder storm ahead of us, so we flew around it and finally landed at Sweetgrass, Montana for customs and on to Cut Bank, Montana for the night.

The next day was quite rough flying under the clouds, so I climbed on top. The clouds gradually got higher and higher, so I climbed to 13,500 ft. I got a headache in the rare air due to diminished oxygen. The rest of the family went to sleep. We landed fine in Spokane for fuel and on to Bellevue through the Cascade Mountains without problems.

Maxine and I flew the Maule to California to look at the possibility to move my residency in surgery to Stockton, CA. We then flew on to Southern California. As we approached VanNuys Airport, we got lost in the smog and found Ventura County Airport far to the west of our destination. They told us to follow the Ventura Freeway to VanNuys. I located the airport and reported downwind in the landing pattern. I got no response from the tower. I reported base with no response. When I turned to the final approach, I heard the tower talking to another plane.

"Hold short. I have a Maule on high final." There are very few Maules, so I knew he was speaking of my plane; and I was tired of flying in smog, so I landed. After a rain, and after visiting relatives, it was CAVU (ceiling and visibility unlimited) when we took off. In Crescent City, California we encountered weather problems; so we left the plane there and took a bus home, as I had to get back to work at the hospital in Seattle. Bob McDowell, another club member, retrieved the plane for me.

In the flying club in Stockton we had a Beach Musketeer and a Piper Tri-Pacer that I flew. The Modesto club had a Piper Super Cub and a Cessna 172. One hot day we decided to fly up to Lake Tahoe for lunch. We took off from Stockton in the Musketeer and climbed up over the Sierra Nevada Mountains toward Donner Pass. It was a slow climb because of four people in the small plane. The first tank of fuel finished and the engine died, but I switched to the other tank right away. However, my friend in the back was frightened and would never fly with me again.

With still a long way to go over the mountains to Lake Tahoe and with less than half the fuel remaining, we decided to go to Sacramento instead. When we arrived it was very hazy. I knew not to land at McClellan Air Force Base. I called Sacramento Airport for directions. He said, "You are right over it." Sure enough! I could see it through the haze; entered the traffic pattern and landed OK. We had a fine lunch and flew back to Stockton.

Then it was off to mission work in Africa. It didn't make sense to make your doctor an air-taxi driver, so I never got a plane to use in the small mountainous country of Burundi. I have flown a bit with my brother Milt in his Aero Commander, but I have not remained current to fly myself.

Incidentally, both Gene and Milt had careers in aviation—Gene in aerial application with helicopters, and Milt in small aircraft and as a flight instructor. Those early years in the flying club gave us a special bond. We three have enjoyed swapping plane stories ever since.

In 2006 we three "boys" had a 50-year reunion at the airport in San Manuel, AZ. We each were taken up for a short flight in a Luscombe of the same type we had flown fifty years before.

50-year reunion with pilot buddies Milt Ogden, Gene VanBrocklin & Frank Ogden beside Luscombe Airplane.

CPSIA information can be obtained
at www.ICGtesting.com
Printed in the USA
LVHW022117151221
706290LV00024B/1354